Paul McKenna's Hypnotic Secrets

Paul McKenna's Hypnotic Secrets

by Paul McKenna, Peter Willis and Clare Staples

BⳆXTREE

DEDICATION
Mum, Dad and brother John, Kenny Everett,
and 'the old master' Peter Casson.

First published in Great Britain in 1995 by Boxtree Limited
Broadwall House · 21 Broadwall · London SE1 9PL

Cover design by Flash & Associates
Book Design by Martin Lovelock and John Round
Printed and bound in the United Kingdom by

Cover photograph by Trevor Leighton
TV Routine photographs by Mark Bourdillon (Carlton UK Television)
Phobias design by Andy White/Woman's Journal/Robert Harding Syndication
Additional photographs by Dave Hogan

Contents

Foreword

NIGEL BENN
World Boxing Council Super Middleweight Champion

'Paul made me believe in myself again; he brought the Dark Destroyer back to life. When I thanked him in the ring after winning my fight against Gerald McClellan, it wasn't for psyching me up, it was for saving my life.

I went to see Paul for a private hypnotism session because my life was falling apart. I was in pieces and I thought I was going to have a nervous breakdown. The pressure became unbearable after I split from my wife Sharron. I was still hopelessly in love with her. I saw her laughing face wherever I went, whatever I was doing. Even when I was fighting the only thing I could think was how much I loved her. Just before Christmas 1994, my agent suggested I saw Paul. I was really sceptical about hypnotism, but as soon as I started talking to Paul I began crying. All that emotion I had kept bottled up for so long just poured out – and I hardly knew the guy.

Paul told me I had to face up to what had happened with my wife and deal with it. I felt like I was Peter Pan floating in and out of clouds. It was the most amazing sensation I've ever felt. I'd never known such peace and tranquillity before. Paul has so much life and energy. When I left Paul's house, the Dark Destroyer had been born again.

He gave me some tapes like Supreme Self Confidence, Motivation Power and Eliminate Stress. Whenever I had a quiet moment at home, I would dim the lights, put on the tapes and listen to everything he said. I was like a different man. I was so relaxed and cool, even when I was training. I felt like nothing could touch me anymore.'

ROBIN SMITH

England cricketer

'Paul McKenna comes with my strongest recommendation because he has been such an enormous help in making my dreams of playing again for England come true. This is the first time I have written about the things he has done for me and I do so in the hope that my story might help others who are perhaps unsure about hypnotism.

I turned to Paul when I was dropped from the England cricket side half way through 1994 after seven consecutive years of playing for them. It came as a shocking blow and the months that followed were the most depressing of my life.

During the dark winter days, I seriously wondered if I would ever play for England again. At 31, a batsman should be starting to reach his peak – but as far as I could see my days of playing top international cricket were over. While I was physically fit, I wasn't so sure about my mental state. One of the things that hindered my career was that I could be too anxious, especially in the first half hour of batting. Really you perform best when you are cool, calm and collected.

After a friend, the comedian Richard Digance, suggested I saw a hypnotist, I got in touch with Paul. Even though I had never been hypnotised before, I badly wanted Paul to help me because I was desperate to get back into England.

I had three hour-long sessions with him which I enjoyed immensely. He made me feel very relaxed, putting me into a hypnotic state to talk to my unconscious mind. I was surprised how easily I went under. Among the areas we worked on were how to perform more confidently under pressure, believe more in my own capabilities, be more comfortable within myself and improve my concentration levels. Generally, he helped me focus better.

Soon afterwards, about nine months after I had been dropped, I was overjoyed to be selected to play in the 1st test match against the West Indies. I will never know what would have happened without Paul, but I found I was more relaxed than I ever had been. My concentration was higher, helping me bat for longer, and I felt quietly more confident when I was required to perform. In fact I was England's top scorer in four consecutive innings in the 2nd and 3rd Test match. Even the cricket commentators congratulated me on my improved performance.

For me the best news of all came when I was selected to play for England in the Test series in South Africa in October 1995, an honour that seemed impossible just 12 months earlier. I hope Paul can help you as much as he has helped me.'

ESTHER RANTZEN

"One of the most dramatic moments I remember on That's Life was the time when Paul helped turn a lady's life around. Muriel Watson had written to tell us that, because of a horrifying side effect of drugs she had been taking after an operation for cervical cancer, she had lost the ability to use her vocal chords properly. It was an awful story. She was hardly able to speak and couldn't even use a phone. Doctors had been unable to help her because there was no actual physical reason why she couldn't speak. It was as if she had forgotten how to walk, she couldn't use her vocal chords properly. We asked Paul if he could help by hypnotising her to use them again properly. It was wonderfully dramatic. She was very husky at first, but she was talking again for the first time in months. We were all very impressed. One of the things it taught me was that hypnosis has a real part to play in medicine because it had such a clear physical effect.

PAULA YATES

TV presenter

"I used to suffer from terribly painful migraines almost every day in 1994. I thought there was nothing I could do about it until a friend suggested I went to see Paul.

I can't remember much about going under, but I do recall that when Paul brought me round I thought he was the most attractive man I'd ever seen. I thought he was Luke Perry!

Seriously though, I went home feeling as though I'd had a two-week holiday in Barbados. It was truly astonishing.

Since I saw him, more than a year ago, I have had about one minor headache. I still can't believe how he helped me. "

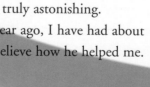

KATE STAPLES

British female pole vault champion
(Zodiac of TV's Gladiators)

I have used Paul's techniques regularly over the past couple of years as, being an international athlete, I've realised that mental fitness is as important as physical fitness. I have a coach to help me be the best I can be physically and I guess I call Paul my mental coach. He helps me reach the optimum peak state I need to be in before a competition. Wherever I am in the world, I call Paul up and he runs through a set of mind exercises which are really fantastic. I think I must be the only one of his clients that he 'does' by telephone but it definitely works for me.

I started pole vaulting when I was 25 which is relatively late to take up a sport like that and I was faced with a variety of people telling me that it was possibly too late. I needed to believe that I could and would beat the current records and Paul certainly cemented that belief in me. The night before I beat the British record for the first time I spent a lot of time with Paul mentally rehearsing the jump which was incredibly helpful.

I believe that hypnosis and sports psychology in general is very underrated in this country. I know that when I travel abroad and meet foreign athletes it is very much an integral part of their training. I think that if people had a better understanding of what exactly hypnosis is and how it works then more people would use it.

BOBBY DAVRO

TV comic

" Paul helped me overcome arachnophobia; for me, a very real debilitating fear of spiders, which had dogged me since one fell on my face when I was about five. I used to be so scared of spiders that even as an adult I couldn't sleep in my house if I knew one was creeping around. I would go running away, screaming like a little girl! Once, after finding one late at night in my kitchen, I had to get a female neighbour to come and get rid of it. She must have thought I was potty.

I thought I would always have to live with the problem until Paul suggested hypnosis. It was amazing. He put me in a trance and got me to look at spiders completely differently, turning them into comical characters. Now when I see one I play the Benny Hill theme tune in my mind and picture the spider wearing silly wellies and looking like Groucho Marx. The ultimate test came when I was given a live tarantula to hold on a children's TV programme recently. Once I would have been panic stricken, but instead my fear had completely vanished. For me, that was quite an achievement – and Paul deserves all my thanks. "

JOAN McKENNA

Paul's mum

" I was pretty sceptical about hypnotism until Paul showed me just how powerful it can be. The most dramatic example came after I had a brain haemorrhage in July 1994. I was in a pretty bad state in hospital, my right hand was paralysed and my words were slurred and addled like I was drunk. I didn't know how long it would last or if it would get worse.

Paul visited me, put me in a trance and asked my subconscious mind if my fingers would move again and when. My subconscious said they would start to move in six days and, amazingly, they did. I was able to move three of my fingers that day which was a wonderful feeling. The other two came the day after.

He left me some of his audio tapes to play which made a huge difference. I played his tape for stress every day for six months and I believe it helped me recover much faster than had been expected. Some people never work again after a brain haemorrhage, but just six months later I went back to my job as an education official. For me, Paul's hypnotism was a miracle. "

Introduction

Nobody has been more astonished than me by the incredible rise in interest in the subject of hypnosis in the 1990s. Although some of the media attention was sensational, most has been positive and incredibly rewarding. Particularly gratifying is the response from viewers of my television shows.

My office receives, on average, two thousand letters a month from all over the world and it has been quite a job at times to keep up with them. It is because of all that mail that I decided to put this book together. My first book, *The Hypnotic World of Paul McKenna*, first published in 1991, is an encyclopaedic overview of the subject whereas I have tailored this book to specifically answer the questions I find I am most often asked. It also gives a unique behind-the-scenes look at how my television show works.

I always felt my audience tended to be people between the ages of 18–35 but at least half of the letters I receive are from children and older people who tell me how fascinated they are by the phenomenon. Some want to try it themselves. While this book does not actually teach how to hypnotise others, I hope it throws much more light on the subject.

Many letters simply ask for help. As well as pointing those people towards my range of hypnotherapy tapes, I can now also offer them the simple, but powerful techniques I have put together in this book aimed at finding personal success, stopping smoking, losing weight, combating stress or even sleeping soundly. They are all proven to be successful – without the need of going into a trance.

Traditionally hypnosis has been steeped in mystery and hypnotists have been keen in the past to imply it is something weird and unusual. I would like to demystify and dispel all the misunderstanding surrounding the subject in as entertaining a way as possible. Although this book is called *Paul McKenna's Hypnotic Secrets*, it would be better in my view if there weren't any. I hope this book goes a long way to answering any questions you have and indeed inspires you to find out more.

Paul McKenna

My Childhood: Early Days

When I was younger I didn't dream of going into showbusiness. I was never showing off in talent contests as a three year old, but on the other hand neither have I ever been exactly shy and retiring.

Looking back to my childhood, I have to respect my parents – Bill, a building contractor, and Joan, an education advisor – for their patience. According to my mother, almost from the day I was born, on 8 November, 1963 (at 8.10am, to be exact), I was a hyperactive handful. She says I was an inquisitive child, always clambering on top of the furniture or running off when I got half a chance. I must have been a terrible influence on my brother John, who is a year-and-a-half younger and now works as a building surveyor.

From early on I always loved practical

(left) 9 weeks old.
(right) At 3, at our home in Enfield. It must have been hard to part me from this bike.

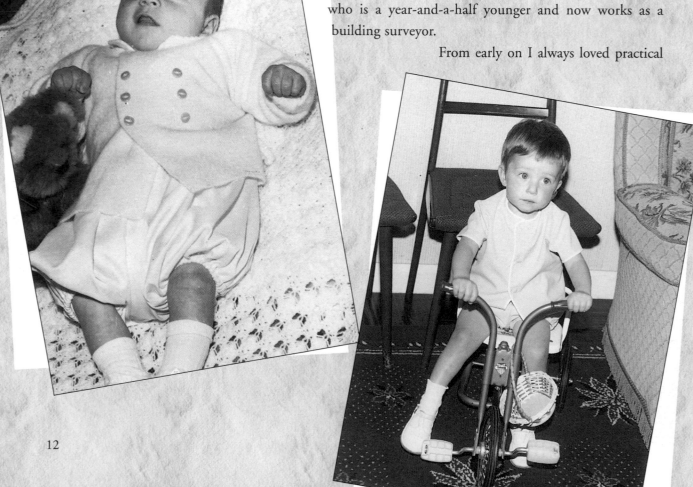

12

joking. The more outrageous the better and, as my family still enjoy reminding me, my own personal safety was never much of a consideration.

On one occasion, when I was about seven, Auntie Gladys was taking John and me for a drive in the country. She was happily tootling along when I scrambled out of the back window, pulled myself over the roof of the car on my stomach, and hung my head over the top of the windscreen, waving at her with a silly grin on my face. I still remember her scream and look of horror. Unfortunately, the last laugh was on me, for she slammed on the brakes, sending me hurtling off the roof and into a ditch. I wasn't seriously hurt, but I was pretty battered and bruised, so I didn't try that again.

My grandfather was another of my targets. There was the time John and I put laxatives in his tea, and once I imitated the voice of a racing commentator on a radio cassette recorder. The shock on his face was a picture when he asked me to turn on the radio for the results – and heard what he thought was the commentator announcing that all his horses had come in second.

That tape machine, a Christmas present when I was 12, was one of the best toys I ever had because it fuelled my ambition to work in radio. I would spend hours on end recording and editing interviews and mixing jingles in my makeshift studio.

It was a shame I didn't know anything about hypnotism when I was a child. There were many times when it would have been useful – particularly for building up my confidence or to the dentist, which terrified me, and to combat my early fear of dogs triggered when one gave me a nasty bite.

(left) Winning a gardening set from Miss Enfield for my impression of Bill ... or was it Ben? (right) Going ape at age 5 with my brother John.

13

SCHOOLDAZE

It was at school that I got my first insight into how easily the mind can be manipulated. I loathed every minute of the miserable six years I spent at a Jesuit boys college.

My teachers, many of them sinister-looking priests who crept around in black cloaks, were in a class of their own at brainwashing. All the time they would tell us we were so wicked, so guilty and so sinful. They instilled the idea that we could never be quite good enough – and all apparently because a long time ago Adam had eaten an apple he wasn't supposed to. I remember it made me so miserable because any of my achievements always seemed tinged with guilt.

Many "educational institutions" use the same techniques as cults, though I wasn't to discover this until years later. They insisted they were telling us the divine truth and everyone else had it wrong. For me it was like being mentally caged in a prison and even when I got home it was hard to lose the feelings of guilt they tried to install in our minds.

Soon after I arrived, aged 11, at St Ignatius College in Enfield, North London I decided the only way to survive was by rebelling. I quickly turned into a bit of a troublemaker who never missed a chance to cause problems to those I perceived as "the enemy". Some friends and I formed ourselves into a secret group we called The Pupils' Revolutionary Party.

(left) Not a happy day. My brother John, left, and I, when I was 15, in our awful school uniforms.
(right) With first double-decks in 1983.

We did all the usual school pranks, regularly let down the teacher's car tyres, etc. One lad in our class vandalised the regal statue of St Ignatius with an open Bible in his hands that stood at the front of the school. He crept back at night, climbed up and superglued the centre spread of *Penthouse* over the Holy book. On another occasion a classmate, who was a black belt in karate, caused a flood by kicking a main water pipe until it burst.

I left school at sixteen with a handful of low grade CSE's which were not much use to anyone. I believe my factory-style education was aimed not so much at instilling knowledge, as teaching us how to conform. I suppose in that respect they failed dismally with me. However, although they had never intended it, the experience did fuel my education in mind control which eventually led to my fascination with hypnosis.

Many of my school friends ended up on the dole or in prison. It was fortunate for me that I had a goal from an early age. I had been determined to make it into radio ever since I heard tapes of the pirate stations.

To me the early king of the pirates Kenny Everett, who was later to become a good friend, was a genius, the George Best of radio. His show on Radio One and later Capital Radio was so inspiring, so refreshingly original and totally unpredictable. He always had that mischievous cheek which frequently got him into trouble. I was amazed by the way he could create a whole world in the imagination of the listener. It has been said that radio is the theatre of the mind. Kenny achieved with words, music and sound effects what many need massive budgets, TV studios and elaborate sets to do.

(left) With Kenny Everett – I'm second from the right.
(right) I looked so grown-up in my first publicity picture at age 17 that when I turned up at Radio One for an interview, they said I looked much younger in the flesh. That was their excuse, anyway!

By fourteen, I had given up my childhood idea of becoming a secret agent and channelled all my energies into becoming a creative radio broadcaster. After writing to Kenny, to my surprise he invited me to watch him on air at Capital Radio's studios in London.

I will never forget how he went out of his way to help me. At the time everyone was trying to copy Kenny, but he gave me some very good advice. He said: "Just remember, whatever you do, the most important thing is to always be original. The public will always prefer an original. A copy will always be second best. You have the raw talent, just keep at it."

So I finally applied myself and after getting five O levels and an A level in art at technical college, I started working as a DJ in Top Shop in London's Oxford Street. I was in heaven, I was 16, working in a fashion store surrounded by beautiful girls and the only work was playing records. I couldn't believe I got paid as well!

Over the next two years I set up a company selling taped music for various stores, but I didn't really enjoy all the paperwork. So, on an impulse I packed my bags and went off to Spain with £50 in my pocket, where I ended up DJ'ing in a disco for the summer. When I returned to England another friend of mine called and asked if I wanted to work on Radio Caroline. It was an illegal pirate station, so a secret meeting was arranged and I got the job. I spent one of the most adventurous times of my life on board a former Icelandic trawler broadcasting from the high seas.

(left) At a family party when I was 22. Who told me streaked hair was trendy?
(right) At Chiltern Radio.

When I came ashore my parents constantly asked when I would get a proper job. However, I was doing what I loved, playing records on the only truly free radio station in Europe. At 21, I finally landed my first real break when I was asked to stand-in for the breakfast DJ on Chiltern Radio. After a few weeks of doing the show it was discovered that the person I was temporarily replacing hadn't gone on holiday, but had been arrested for drug smuggling! The bosses were so overwhelmed with embarrassment they didn't start interviewing for a replacement, but took me on full-time.

It was a decision they probably came to regret. Inspired by the American shock jocks like Howard Stern, I managed to boost the morning figures through constant controversy. One of my favourite memories is getting commuters in the regular tailbacks on the M1 to blast their car horns in protest. It created a 14 mile, ear-bursting cacophony of noise, an incident which was even reported in *The Daily Telegraph*.

I loved to conjure up images in people's minds through the radio and I suppose that helped me to become a wordsmith of sorts. I wasn't to know it at the time, but I realise now that radio, which is essentially all about language and communication, was the perfect training ground for a hypnotist.

(left) Life in the fast lane. Go-karting in 1990.
(right) I would get people to send me chain-letters so I could tear them up on air.

Mesmerised

How did I become interested in hypnosis? Why did I leave a successful career in radio broadcasting to pursue this apparently strange interest? It all began when I was 23, working as the breakfast show DJ on Chiltern Radio, a local commercial station based in Hertfordshire. I had been reading lots about hypnosis and one day interviewed a local hypnotist, a nutty professor type. As part of the piece, I asked him to hypnotise me and I was amazed at the profound changes in my consciousness during the experience.

I had been feeling very stressed, but woke up feeling so good, rested and relaxed and quite euphoric. What's more the sensation lasted for three days. I was amazed by the effect it had on me. Since the age of 18, I had been into personal development, Zen, meditation, yoga and some of the alternative medicines, partly, I believe, as a reaction to my Jesuit education.

Now with hypnotism, I had found something even more mindblowing which excited me more than anything I had studied before. I loved it and was instantly hooked. I persuaded the hypnotist to lend me some of his dusty, old, leather-bound books to read up on how the mind works. I started finding out as much as I could about the subject; reading books, watching hypnotherapy videos and going to see stage hypnotists.

One night I was watching a show when, after about 20 minutes, I felt I had unlocked the secret of exactly how the subjects were put into a trance. When this vital piece of the jigsaw was added, I could see the whole picture – suddenly all the theory I had read made sense. I began practising on friends – with increasing success. A few days later I told my first brave subject, a DJ colleague called Tony West, that when he woke up he would believe an object I gave him was a valuable antique.

I handed him a squeezy bottle before saying my familiar: "Wakey, wakey, rise and shine". When I asked what he was holding, he said, with total conviction: "It's a beautiful vase – a precious heirloom that has been in the family for more than a century." Later I gave him a suggestion that when he stepped onto the kitchen floor he would be convinced it was hot. He immediately started jumping about and, as I tried to contain my laughter, I woke him up. I am not sure which of us was more surprised, Tony because he had been hypnotised or me because I had hypnotised him!

To turn the tables, I got someone to try putting me into a relaxing trance by using the words of my script – "Relax your eyes, now relax your mouth … ". Then, to test how effective it had been, I got him to suggest that the back of my hand was numb before he jabbed it with a pin. It worked. I was so relaxed I felt no pain at all. (Don't try this at home!)

I quickly realised that, apart from just entertainment, hypnosis was the most powerful psychological tool I had ever come across to really help people instantly overcome fears and phobias and for lasting dramatic change. First I attempted to stop a couple of friends from smoking – and to my astonishment it worked. Next I got a call from my next door neighbour's son who had a biology mock O-level exam the next day. He felt that he hadn't done enough revision and was acutely anxious about the exam.

I put him into trance and gave him some simple direct suggestions such as : "When you wake up tomorrow you will be able to remember all you need to know for your exams, the information will easily come into your mind." The next day after school he came round and said: "What did you do to me? I could remember everything." I thought I had just made him more confident and was sure that he had probably written total garbage, thinking he knew the answers.

Weeks later when the results came through, he had failed everything – all except his biology in which he had got an A. Sadly for him, because he had done very little work that year, his teacher thought he had been cheating!

I realised that having an understanding of hypnotism is like having an owner's manual for the brain. When you really begin to use your own incredible bio-computer more efficiently anything is possible. I believe if hypnotism could be bottled, it would be the most powerful drug in the world.

PAUL McKENNA

MUSIC POWER

CAPITAL RADIO 95·8FM STEREO

Trance

The word 'trance' conjures up visions of sleepwalking Zombies. But trance is something we all experience every day. Watching TV or sitting in a cinema are both similar to being in a trance. We literally suspend belief in the outside world and concentrate on what's happening on the screen. It's not real, just tiny coloured dots moving to create images, but the more we become absorbed the more real it seems.

A hypnotist uses his skills to set off these changes of consciousness to deliberately create this daydream state of fascination; it's called a hypnotic trance. Hypnotism by-passes the conscious, critical, analytical mind. So someone in a trance can become fixated on one idea or suggestion to the virtual exclusion of everything else. It's rather like an actor losing himself in a part.

Self-hypnosis is an excellent way of relaxing and solving problems. The secret is just to let it happen; everyone learns at their own speed. Avoid over-analysing and instead simply relax, notice and enjoy the experience. Everyone can do it although people who suffer from epilepsy, clinical depression or any other psychiatric problem should not attempt self-hypnosis. If in doubt just ask your doctor.

There are many different ways to do self-hypnosis – in its most simple form it's just daydreaming. Einstein, for example, imagined what riding on a beam of light would be like and from this daydream he came up with the theory of relativity. Trance is a unique experience, but it's important to find a time and place where you can safely and comfortably relax for about 20 minutes – turn off the phone or ask not to be disturbed. Obviously, don't do hypnotic trance while driving or using any machinery!

Before you start make yourself physically comfortable. Decide the purpose of your trance – relaxation, energy boosting, confidence, sports improvement, whatever. Be as precise as you can because the more clearly you state your desired outcome the more likely you are to get it.

Set a time limit. Say: 'I'm going to relax into trance only as deeply as I need to and vividly imagine, for example, giving my speech confidently and perfectly at the wedding. I will imagine it five times to really let my unconscious mind learn what I want to happen. When I awaken from trance after 15 minutes I will be refreshed, relaxed, alert and feeling more confident."

Next create a "safety statement". Tell yourself that if for any reason or emergency you need to awaken you will wake up immediately. There are many ways of doing it, just experiment until you find the way that's right for you.

Systematic Relaxation Induction

This is the easiest and most popular technique. Simply close your eyes and, one stage at a time, relax each part of your body. It helps to talk to yourself in a progressively slower rhythmic monotone as you relax each part. Like this :

Now I relax my eyes,

Now I relax my mouth,

Now I relax my neck,

Now I relax my shoulders,

Now I relax my arms,

Now I relax my chest,

Now I relax my stomach,

Now I relax my legs,

Now I relax my feet.

Mental Rehearsal

Once you feel relaxed you can vividly imagine yourself winning a race or giving a successful presentation, or just calming beautiful scenery. Whatever it is that you want to achieve or that makes you feel good, imagine it as clearly as you can. Don't see yourself in the image, but instead look out through your eyes and see what you'll see as you achieve what you want.

When you are thinking of something good it helps to make the image in your mind bigger. Expand it, make the colours brighter and the sounds louder as this in turn makes the good feelings stronger.

The Betty Erickson Induction

Here is my favourite way of inducing self-hypnosis. It was invented by Betty Erickson, Milton Erickson's wife (see page 66). I find it particularly good for problem solving. Once you have stated your safety suggestion and set a time limit, state what the problem is that you want to solve. Say something like: "I'm going to relax into trance and allow the wisdom of my unconscious mind to come up with creative ideas to help me understand how to best get on with Frank, or win the contract, or come up with good ideas for my presentation" (or whatever else you want). See how well it works for you:

1 Find something to focus on such as a spot on the ceiling. Then make four statements about what you see, in a rhythmic, progressively slower, monotonous tone of voice in your head. For instance: "Now I can see books, Now I can see the floor, Now I can see the wall, the cuffs of my shirt."

2 Make four statements to yourself about what you can hear. "I can hear the traffic passing, I can hear my breathing, the clock ticking, birds singing."

3 Make four statements about what you can feel. "I feel the weight of my body in the chair, my facial muscles relaxing, the warmth of my hands, the movement of my shirt over my chest."

4 Then go back and make three statements about what you see. It doesn't matter if you repeat yourself. Then make three statements about what you hear and three about what you feel.

5 Go round again, making two statements. When your eyes feel tired, close them but carry on making statements – what you describe will come from your imagination now.

6 Round again, making one statement. If you get to the bottom of the list and your conscious mind is still active, go back to the top creating ever finer distinctions.

HOW I HYPNOTISE A SUBJECT

This is an outline of how I relax people into a trance and help them with hypnotherapy.

1 I establish rapport with the subject by matching my emotional mood to hers. I begin by giving indirect suggestions, explaining what the subject can expect and pacing her expectations. I tell her how easy, natural and enjoyable the whole experience will be.

2 I tell her to fix her attention on something such as a spot on the ceiling. In the old days hypnotists used a swinging watch.

3 After a while the subject's eyelids become heavy and I give her a suggestion to close them.

4 Then I suggest progressive relaxation. I tell the subject to relax her facial muscles, shoulders, chest, stomach, legs, arms. The subject's facial muscles begin to relax along with the rest of her body. Sometimes there is a change in skin colour or breathing pattern which becomes slower and more rhythmic.

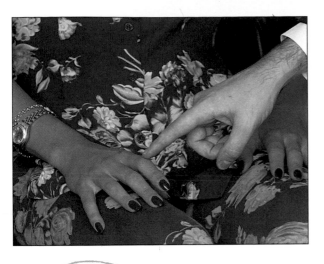

5 Once the subject is in a trance, I speak to her unconscious mind. I ask for a response to my questions, using finger movement, telling her to place her hands on her lap and raise one finger to indicate yes and another for no.

6 In this case I ask the subject's unconscious mind if she can make changes which will be helpful to her. I ask her to make a positive change.

7 She raises the finger which we had decided will mean yes, indicating she agrees to do that.

8 I offer the subject some general suggestions for her wellbeing and happiness before I awaken her.

9 Then I bring her out of trance, counting back from ten to one and finally instructing her to awaken feeling refreshed and alert.

Using Hypnosis for Success

I haven't always been such a confident person. I know what it's like to feel really depressed. When I was about 22, I found I was not enjoying my job at Chiltern Radio any more, I hated my boss, my workload was leaving me mentally and physically drained and, to cap it all, my then girlfriend dumped me. Everything seemed to have stacked up against me, driving me to the edge of despair.

As I was driving back home one night, mulling it all over, I just couldn't see any hope for myself. For one insane moment I thought all my problems would be solved by driving off the edge of a cliff. Fortunately I saw sense that night but, without doubt, that was the lowest point of my life.

It is hard to believe that I ever felt so bad, worthless and unfulfilled, but now, around a decade later, I am glad to say it could never happen again because quite simply I don't get depressed anymore. I have since discovered a variety of hypnotic techniques which make life very fulfilling. I may get angry, sometimes frustrated, but never depressed.

At the time I was performing my hypnotic show at small venues in breaks from working on the radio. One day I sat down, put myself into a trance, and imagined my life five years on – I didn't like what I saw. My picture of myself was that I was more paranoid, worrying about young DJ's joining the station, no *richer* and, worse, no *happier*.

I knew that wasn't what I wanted so I asked myself to imagine where I would *really* like to be in five years. I visualised a career as a hypnotist, a show on TV, my own audiotapes, a beautiful girlfriend, a lovely house in London and enough money to do the things I wanted … The events I witnessed in the future have incredibly unfolded in my life as if by clockwork but I am convinced that this was because I committed myself 100% per cent to making as much of the *visualisation* as possible come true.

With such a compelling future to look forward to, I instantly became more enthusiastic and *motivated*. I realised I would have to become knowledgeable about hypnosis so I spent up to six hours a day studying and practising the subject.

I then decided to take my biggest risk to date to make things happen. I began investing every penny into staging increasingly larger shows. It was a dangerous, but calculated, gamble. From the moment I created that visualisation of my future I kept a vivid picture in my mind of who I wanted to be – then I did everything I could to make sure that I gradually became that person.

It is true that if you believe in yourself, have *confidence* in yourself, then others believe in you too. It is rather like a self-fulfilling prophesy. I firmly believe you get back from life what you put into it. So in the same way it is just as important what message you send out. I started to put out more *positive energy* and I certainly began to get it back.

At all costs I wanted to avoid thinking negatively. I went on what I called a 'negative thought fast'. Every time I caught myself thinking negatively about someone or something I used a simple technique. I would see the negative picture in my mind and then I would literally play with it in my *imagination*. I would drain all the colour out of it, shrink the picture and spin it off into space and then simply replace it with a positive picture of something that feels good.

At the same time I decided to change the way I felt about money. Up until then, I had always been trying to make ends meet. Every time a bill arrived I would feel bad, my stomach muscles would tighten. I had a very old and scruffy plastic cheque book holder, with book to match, which certainly reflected the state of my disorganised finances. I decided to *visualise* wealth. I pretended to myself I had thousands in the bank so when I opened bills, I looked at them completely differently. By doing this I was sending a new message to my unconscious mind.

One afternoon I even went as far as cutting up one of my bank statements and rearranging the overdrawn figures into a different order until it showed I was thousands in credit. I remember laughing so hard as I was sticking it together. I know it sounds really strange now but it gave me a very strong sense of what it might feel like to have that amount of money in the bank.

I went on to make a scrap book of all the things that I wanted from life. It even included pop stars I wanted to interview such as David Byrne from the Talking Heads and Ricky Ross from Deacon Blue. The weird thing was that within a week I got phone calls offering me an interview with Ricky Ross, and a couple of nights later David Byrne walked into the studio.

I think the most valuable lesson from this is the importance of goal setting. I effectively just combined that simple concept with self-hypnosis to make it more powerful.

The famous American Evangelist Rev. Robert Shuller is right when he says: 'Failing to plan is a plan to fail."

Your step by step guide to doing it for yourself

STEP ONE: What do you really want?

If you are not clear about what you want then you are putting vagueness out into the world and that is all you will get back. One of the most important steps is to develop your ability to think through and decide upon what you really desire.

All of the really successful individuals I have worked with have this skill in abundance. Some of them always did it naturally, others learned to do it – I will explain how.

It begins in the imagination. The best goal setters and planners have a strong ability to imagine things that haven't happened but could. For anything to happen in the real, external world it has to happen in the internal world of your imagination first.

Some people are afraid to write down what they want because they think it will somehow commit them to taking action. Success frightens them. Others avoid 'thinking on paper' because they never follow through on written plans, so why bother?

I believe it's important to take the time to write down your ideas and imaginings when considering what you want to do so you can sit back from *what* you are thinking about and evaluate *how* you are thinking.

If you would like to achieve great benefits from life, you will need to take a few minutes and think through some of the goals you would like to achieve. Perhaps there are dreams that you would like to realise but haven't as yet taken any action on. Another way to think about this is: 'What would success in my life involve or what would I do if I knew I couldn't fail?'

Or ask yourself this; is there anything in your career, health, relationships, finances that you are not happy about? If so, how would you like it to be?

Go into a vivid daydream and see what comes to mind.

STEP 2: Brainstorm

Now write down what it is that you really want.

Ask yourself: What would I have if I could have anything I wanted? What possessions would I want, what abilities, what kind of people around me, what kind of experiences?

This is something that you can do regularly. Next you need to ask yourself : What is a reasonable time within which to have those things happen – a month, a year?

STEP 3: Who will you have to become?

Next ask yourself who will you have to become to fulfil those goals – what new skills will you have to learn, what character traits will you have to develop, who will you need to know?

When I started this process years ago, I soon realised that I would have to dress differently, rather than in jeans and t-shirts all the time. I would have to invest in some suits because I would be perceived differently – something I had never properly considered before.

In order to steer into a new successful direction a simple, but important thing like dress can change the course of your life. I also realised I would need to educate myself about the mind and modern psychology together with learning some advanced rapport and communication skills. Another thing I had to change was my self-confidence level.

It's also important to ask yourself : What will having what I want do for me? What will it really give me?

A man at one of my seminars told me that all he had ever wanted was money, so I asked him how would that make him feel. He thought about it before eventually answering that it would make him feel more secure. So, security, rather than actual cash, was what he wanted in the end. There I was able to help because it's easy to create feelings of total security.

During the seminar he learned how to re-programme himself to feel more secure. This gentleman wrote to me a few months later telling me how much better he felt about who he was, the money seemed less important but he had actually started to make more of it. He concluded that by healing his self image and the insecurity scars within he had effectively steered his mind to what he'd truly wanted. He'd changed within himself so in turn the world outside had changed.

STEP 4: Rehearsal Success

It is important to vividly imagine living your goals. Run through your ideal day, from morning to night. The more vividly you can make your images and sounds the better.

To feel more positive, you need to think of times in the past that you have been very positive. This is called positive mental rehearsal and it's what successful Olympic athletes do to put them in a positive state of mind before competing. By imagining success over and over again, they train their minds to expect success so unconsciously they begin to attract it to them like a magnet, more and more every day.

Applying these same techniques, not only will you feel better, but you will be guiding yourself in the direction you really want to go. By visualising, you send a strong message to your unconscious mind which is essentially all your wisdom and creativity – all your true potential.

Don't worry if you have failures along the way. I find it's more helpful to see failure as feedback because that's all it really is. As the man who started IBM said, "If you want to double your success rate, first you have to be prepared to double your failure rate."

STEP 5: Scrapbook

Make a scrapbook of pictures of the things you want . You can also give yourself the experiences you want to have. One of my friends, as well as visualising, actually test drove several Mercedes so he could really get a sense of the feel of the car, the smell of the leather, the joy it would give him to own one.

One of the golden rules in success conditioning that I cannot emphasise enough is *you always get more of what you focus on*. Some people sabotage themselves by always thinking of what they don't want. 'I don't want to be fat' they say, 'If only I wasn't so fat,' or 'How can I not be fat?' It's like saying try not to think of the colour blue! In order to 'not' something you have to think of it, so when using the techniques in this book usually it's best to think of what you *do* want rather than what you don't.

In a nutshell, I believe you have to be successful in the privacy of your own mind over and over again because you always get more of what you focus on in life. Condition yourself for success.

STEP 6: Resources

Make a list of every single thing in your life that you could possibly consider a resource.

Contacts – think of everyone you know and who in turn they know. Clothes, skills, things that you do, your looks. Your brain is an incredible resource – it can come up with all kinds of incredibly creative ideas. Where you live – the Western World – is an extremely wealthy and happening place to be. The media gives you information and that means power. Include everything from your car to your health, even little things like pens and pencils mean you can write.

When I did this several years ago my list went on for ten pages. It's an exercise I always recommend. Not only will it make you feel more resourceful, but it points your mind in the direction of seeing how those resources can best be used to help you achieve your goals.

Remember only you can do it. Things will change as you put in the effort. So make a commitment to yourself to do the techniques everyday.

Start now!

On Tour
from Village Hall to Albert Hall

The phenomenal surge of interest in hypnotism has, of course, delighted me. More than 250,000 people saw my live hypnotic stage show at one of the 200 dates around the world in 1994. At least 2,000 of them didn't just sit and watch, but volunteered to take part as the stars of the show – making every performance unique.

I am proud of the figures, especially as Britain's top promoter Harvey Goldsmith told me that more people saw the show live in Britain than had watched one of the world's biggest rock bands U2 in one year. He also told me that I had played to more people than the Rolling Stones. I was chuffed until I realised they didn't tour that particular year!

Yet it still feels like only yesterday when I made that first performance in front of just 50 people in a small provincial pub. Friends had been urging me to 'go professional' for some time and I was aware that there was certainly a demand after presenting increasingly popular cabaret style routines at parties.

I took the plunge in 1987 – a couple of friends lent me their local pub The DeFrevell Arms in Cambridge for a Sunday night with just a handful of extremely sceptical regulars, paying £1 a head. They were there not knowing what to expect – most had nothing better to do – but they must have reported favourably to their friends because the following Sunday the audience had shot up to 100. And the week after that the pub was so jammed I had to cut the show short for safety reasons.

It was then that the tremendous potential of the show hit me and I knew I had to take it to a considerably bigger venue. I had spent months going along to a lot of different hypnotic shows. While all were slightly different most of the hypnotists seemed to delight in getting laughs through humiliation.

I wanted to bring my show to a completely new family audience by performing in theatres. I could see that people, even those normally shy and reserved, would be keener to take part because rather than the audience laughing *at* them they would be laughing *with* them.

So, with more than a little trepidation, I hired the 800 seater Queensway Hall in Dunstable, Beds in January 1988 for my first real hypnotic stage show. Commercially, it was hardly in the Lloyd Webber league. In fact, after advertising costs, I didn't make

a penny. But, that didn't matter because I was fired up with excitement, realising the vast potential of it all.

I was booked to perform at Army and RAF bases, village halls, prestigious clubs and, most gratifying of all, at the annual Oxford and Cambridge University Summer Balls. (See picture above.) The show always went down a storm there – not least because the students made such excellent subjects. As a result of their intelligence, the responses were guaranteed to be not only remarkably inventive, but hilariously funny too. Of course it was also fun to see the country's creme de la creme – perhaps some of our future leaders – strutting like Mick Jagger or talking in gobbledegook "Martian".

But, much as I loved the shows, I was unsure about exactly where to go with hypnosis – especially as my radio career was taking off, having a landed a job as a DJ with Capital Radio in London.

To help plot my future, I sat down one day and made a list of all my resources – I had a car, a telephone, a way of communicating to millions of Londoners, contacts and worked for an organisation which promoted concerts, and so on. Then, walking through the West End, the next day it suddenly went off in my head like a lightbulb that I should be staging my shows at Capital's very own theatre, the Duke Of York's.

After the station's boss Richard Park gave me his backing, I had to find £5,000 to pay for posters, staff and deposit for the hire of the theatre for six nights before Christmas 1989. Somehow I talked the bank manager into giving me a loan; when I told him it was for a hypnotism show he seemed very suspicious, but probably agreed thinking that if he didn't he'd soon be clucking like a chicken! I was very well aware that if the whole project nose dived it could take me a whole year to pay back.

Not surprisingly, I worried before the show. We just did everything we could to make sure we sold at least 75% of the 650 tickets. And I mean everything. I went out in the dead of the night, every night, pasting up show posters all over London. I dropped off piles of leaflets in every hotel in the West End and I stuck them over every notice board at public buildings including the Royal Free Hospital, right next to posters about the latest medical breakthroughs.

It was with a mixture of fear and excitement that I stepped onto the stage of the Duke Of York's one Sunday evening in December 1989 – becoming only the second hypnotist to perform in the West End in 40 years. Most hypnotists had been put off by having to apply for a licence to perform. I always think it's amusing that the only other people who need such permission are lion tamers!

Unfortunately, despite driving myself into the ground promoting the show, I still lost £100 on the big night – though there was an impressively large turn-out of doctors and nurses!

Undeterred, I got my picture taken standing next to the 'house full' sign outside the theatre. It may sound silly, but the purpose was to spur me on. I concentrated on it every day for three weeks until it became true. Concentrating on the picture gave me a rush of ideas about how to get people to the theatre.

As word spread, ticket sales steadily rose so that by the end of the run we were hitting full houses. The run turned over £36,000 – and yet had not made a penny in profit. But I knew we had got a great show which had really created a buzz. People such as Barry Humphries, Lenny Henry, Dawn French and Ruby Wax as well as a lot of magicians and other variety performers, had come down to see what all the fuss was about.

Some of the stars and of course many cynical journalists were convinced it was fixed, suggesting that the subjects were paid stooges. All I can say is that if that were true I would be broke with debts from having to pay hush money to all the thousands who have taken part. And where would I find them all to hire in the first place?

Perhaps the most important visitor for me was top promoter Harvey Goldsmith. He instantly loved the show, offered to represent me and moved me to another West End theatre that was four times larger.

The Dominion seemed to me to be far too big, with a capacity of 2,500. But we put on five shows in the middle of 1990 – and they sold out immediately. I was thrilled. Many of the audience came back week after week, knowing that every show is different. In fact in 1994 we celebrated the 1000th show – that's a total audience of around 200,000.

Undoubtedly the highlight touring was performing the world's biggest ever live hypnotic show in front of an audience of 5,500 at London's Royal Albert Hall in 1992. To get me in the right state of mind for this important show, I stood backstage and focused my attention upon confidence. I imagined a time when I felt really confident, a time when I thought I couldn't fail. I remembered what I felt like, where I was and when I had a clear sense of the feeling I squeezed my finger and thumb together associating the feeling to a physical 'anchor'. Then I imagined the

(above) On stage at a summer ball.

show going really well and fired the confidence anchor off, creating a feeling of certainty about the show. It worked brilliantly that night and really is one of the single most powerful techniques I know to quickly change the way you feel.

Over the years I have been performing my stage shows there have been a lot of memorable incidents. I remember doing one show when someone I didn't particularly get on with at school came on stage. He took great delight in telling the entire audience what he thought of me as a youngster before writing the show off as rubbish and that he could never be hypnotised.

Unfortunately for him he went out like a light and I gave him the suggestion for the rest of the evening that he would think I was the nicest guy in the world. He spent

'The Boss' ... thanks to Clare.

The night I first performed at The Royal Albert Hall everybody had come along to support me. All the most important people in my personal and professional life, the people that had helped me reach that pinnacle in my career. At the end of the show my stage manager handed me a list of people to thank, people behind the scenes that rarely get the credit but without whom I wouldn't be where I am today. I made a small speech acknowledging all their hard work and occasionally glanced at the list to make sure I hadn't missed anyone out. Unfortunately for me the person that handed me the list had omitted to put her own name on the list and as a result I never mentioned her in my acknowledgements. I would therefore like to take this opportunity to make up for that oversight.

I was performing a show in Guildford in May 1991 when Clare Staples walked on stage. She immediately caught my attention mainly because her hair didn't seem quite right. As the evening wore on it slowly dawned on me, as well as the audience, that she was actually wearing a wig. Eventually, as the routines became more energetic the wig started to slip and she ducked offstage to take it off altogether. When she came back on to the stage she revealed, not a bald scalp, but more blonde hair, which certainly had me puzzled.

It was only later she explained to me she had come with a famous friend, Annabel Croft, who hadn't wanted to be recognised being hypnotised, so they had both worn wigs as a joke. Clare was a brilliant subject. As has been widely reported, I hypnotised her to think I was Mel Gibson, clearly stretching her imagination a little! Despite the usefulness of such an exercise, I, of course, brought her out of the trance at the end of the show. Even though I was instantly attracted to Clare ethics prevented me from asking her out that night.

Fortunately, we discovered that we had a mutual friend and he initiated another meeting at a friend's party where we hit it off. I think her mum and sister Kate, took a little more convincing. I remember them eyeing me particularly suspiciously when we first met, clearly thinking that I still had Clare under some sort of strange spell.

the entire show complimenting me, asking if he could buy me a drink, and to drop in if ever I was in his area.

Another night one of the subjects revealed he was a tax inspector and I gave him a suggestion that everyone in the audience was Lester Piggot. He spent the whole of the interval running about lecturing people on the penalties of false accounting and trying to find out where they were hiding all their money.

At one show the police came backstage and told us that they were investigating a bomb threat near to the Dominion Theatre. They didn't want to let the audience out into what could be a dangerous area and they asked me to announce there was a bomb scare and for everybody to stay inside the theatre until it was declared safe to

Clare had some experience in public relations and I asked her if she would like to see what she could for me. She literally threw herself headlong into doing anything she could to make me successful. She made my self-esteem soar. She instantly rearranged my office in my small home in Enfield, Middlesex, and began promoting me amongst party organisers. She re-designed and re-wrote my show programme, and helped me enormously with research for my first book, patiently re-typing my nonsensical ramblings!

Clare also set about smartening up my appearance, which meant the painful destruction of all my freebie record company t-shirts which I had lived in up to then. She also took a long hard look at my stage show and came up with some great ideas for it. With remarkable foresight, she thought it should be aimed much more at a family audience. She set about thinking up more imaginative and adventurous routines which really transformed my act.

Just as importantly, she changed my values. At the time I was turning into a 'hypno-anorak' who spent every spare minute of the day reading or watching videos about the powers of the mind. Clare made me a much nicer person, far less consumed with ambition. After two years of working together I eventually asked Clare to officially become my personal manager and it really has proved to be a fantastic partnership. She has been far more valuable to me than any hypnosis.

leave. I pointed out that if we weren't careful there would be a terrible panic. We decided instead to just keep the show going until we got clearance from the police but it proved more difficult than we had thought. The show just went on and on as I waited for the all clear. I began running out of routines and started thinking I'd have to start doing them all over again.

As we went into the third hour, I knew the poor audience were wondering if the show were ever going to finish. To make it worse, some people, desperate to catch the last bus home, were sent back to their seats. Thankfully, the area was declared safe just before any trouble started.

Another evening Olympic champion and prankster Daley Thompson, a good friend, popped backstage just before a show. Standing in the wings, he casually turned to me and asked how long it would be before the curtain went up. I told him we had exactly a minute. Daley ran to the centre of the stage, dropped his trousers – and bared his bottom in the direction of where the audience were waiting for the show to start.

As we convulsed with laughter, he then counted down sixty seconds only pulling his trousers up and rushing off as the curtain was going up. He was lucky – the raising of the curtain was actually programmed into a computer and if he had been just a few seconds out, the audience would have one more thing to laugh about at the start of the show.

Since the TV series has now been seen in so many countries, it has been a great opportunity to take the live show around the world. In 1994 it was time to undertake my first international tour – eight weeks through Australia, New Zealand and Hong Kong.

It was a long trip and certainly had its ups and downs, almost putting me and the crew off touring ever again.

It started better than we could have hoped in Australia. Unknown to us Take That were in town for a concert and they seemed to be doing the same publicity rounds as us. At every radio and TV station we were greeted by groups of hysterical screaming girls which was fine by me. As Take That had never been there before I think the fans must have been a little confused as everytime me and my motley crew arrived in our limo they would all start screaming. Some even fainted.

One night in Christchurch I was right in the middle of putting the subjects into trance when an enormous earthquake struck. The chandeliers rattled, the floor rolled and the theatre literally shook. Some of them opened their eyes, nervously wondering what on earth was happening. Realising that if everybody woke up, I would have to start the induction right from the beginning, I turned to them and said, "If you don't go into trance, I'll do that again." I've never seen a group go into trance quicker!

Working one-to-one

This is my study where I hypnotise most of the subjects who see me privately for one-to-one therapy sessions. I try to see as many people as I can from the hundreds of letters I receive every week. These days sadly I have so little time because of the demands of my other projects but on a good week my diary is filled with as many as ten individual sessions.

On arrival, I invite them to sit in the large leather winged chair which dominates the room. Behind the chair is a CD player and a selection of discs which I sometimes turn to during the sessions. For arachnophobia, for example, I might play a CD of the funny Benny Hill theme tune, while asking the subject to imagine a spider. By mixing happy feelings with the fear, the terror is diminished. I have found it to be a highly successful technique.

As I said, because of pressure of time, I am no longer able to see everyone who requests a session with me, but I still try to squeeze in as many private hypnotherapy sessions as I can, and they are certainly not all with celebrities. Each one lasts around an hour, depending on the problem. Most of them are for help in straightforward areas such as boosting confidence, stopping smoking or curing phobias.

However, I have also treated one or two unusual cases. One man had a particularly embarrassing compulsion to stick his tongue out in moments of anxiety, such as meetings! There are many people, of course, who have no specific problems, but simply want to perform to the optimum. For example athletes who want to move faster, bat better and score more often.

Because I find working with people very rewarding, I probably enjoy these sessions more than any other aspect of my work. I don't charge a fee but I do ask my clients to give a donation to their favourite charity. I feel very lucky to have had all the success I've had, and this is one way that I can give something back.

TOP TEN REASONS FOR VISITING A GOOD HYPNOTHERAPIST

1 Lack of Confidence
2 Stop smoking
3 Slimming
4 Insomnia
5 Stress
6 Public speaking
7 Phobias
8 Speech Problems
9 Self Improvement
10 Learning difficulties

SUCCESSFUL SLIMMING

I've noticed something really strange about people who go on diets to lose weight – they think about food all the time! In fact it seems as though the only time they don't think about food is when they are eating – then they try not to admit what they are doing. I think that is pretty unhelpful and, what is more, it doesn't work.

To lose weight, to have a good healthy bodyweight you have to do better than that. After all when you look good and feel good you want to enjoy yourself, right? That means enjoying food, not being obsessive about it.

So this is how to get there. You have to prepare your mind and body for being slim now. Nearly all diets get you into a fight with your body and nearly all people who think they are fat hate their bodies. The secret to losing weight and staying slim and healthy is co-operating with your body and using its intelligence. You have a

MY SIX POINT PLAN FOR SUCCESSFUL SLIMMING

1 Create a positive body image. Imagine standing in front of a mirror and see the body you want to have reflected back at you. Look at it, get to know every inch of it. When you have visualised it really clearly imagine walking into the mirror world and stepping into your future body – feel in yourself the smooth muscles, the trim figure and fit lively feeling and realise that every minute of the day you are heading towards this figure. This is your true self, a body you can be proud of.

2 Be totally aware of every mouthful of food you eat. Notice its taste and texture, its temperature and shape in your mouth, and feel it passing down into your stomach. And notice all the different feelings in your stomach as you eat.

3 Whenever you are not enjoying what you are eating, STOP. The moment you are not totally enjoying every aspect of your food, your body is telling you it is not right for you now. If you were starving, stale bread would taste delicious – because your body would need to eat whatever it could get to stay alive – but when you are well-fed even delicious food isn't totally enjoyable if your body doesn't need it. So learn to listen to all the signals from your body, and as soon as your stomach signals, it has had enough, as soon as your tastebuds tell you "this isn't fun anymore" – STOP eating.

4 Eat fresh food whenever possible. Factory products, such as pre-prepared meals and tinned food, contain additives and very often sugar. Sugar confuses your body – and as a general rule the more you eat the more difficult it is for your body to balance your nutrition. If you have a craving for sugar, eat some wholemeal bread. Your body will be satisfied

40

natural bodyweight, just as you have a natural height. If you are overweight you have over-ridden your body's natural control system.

When your body has had enough it lets you know – you get a sense of 'being full' in your stomach. It is possible to over-ride that feeling but if you do your body believes you are doing it for a good reason, for example that famine is coming. So your body lets your stomach expand so you eat more and stores as much of the energy that it can as fat, so you'll make it through the famine. But we don't have famines in the Western world these days, so when you feel full don't over-ride that feeling because you send the wrong signals to your body.

My six-point plan for losing weight teaches you to listen to your body's wisdom and co-operate with it, so you lose weight, stay slim and get on with enjoying your life. Some people might eat too much because they are stressed or unhappy. If that's true of you then look at my six-points on stress on pages 62-63 and my plan on goal setting for success on pages 26-31. But you know losing weight and looking good are great for your self-esteem. So sort out the other elements of your life, but don't put off losing weight.

Follow these six points and gradually, steadily, you will lose weight until you reach your natural fit body weight and you feel better than you ever have in your life. Enjoy it!

with it and the less sugar you eat the less you seem to want it.

5 Forget about diets, calories and deprivation. If thinking and counting actually lost you weight you would have got slim years ago. You have got to let your body teach you what it really wants. If you follow all the other points in this programme you will lose weight. You are learning to eat with your mouth and your stomach, not your eyes. You stop eating when you have had the right amount of food for you – not when the plate is empty.

6 Take exercise. Use your newly fit body, that's what its muscles are there for. Fat people don't just dislike their bodies, they don't use them either. But when you are slim and healthy you have fit strong muscles which are there to be used. Some people say you have to take exercise to lose weight, but they've got it the wrong way round. The point is if you lose weight you have to take exercise, because your body is prepared to work now it is fit – and you'll feel great when you do it. Start gently, of course, and you don't have to become an athlete. If you just cycle to work, go swimming a couple of times a week or take up tennis or any other sport, you are sending a signal to your body that you want to use it so it should stay fit and healthy.

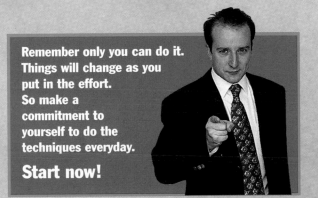

Remember only you can do it. Things will change as you put in the effort. So make a commitment to yourself to do the techniques everyday.

Start now!

On TV - from the West End to the Hypnotic World

While it was my goal to have a TV show, it took so long to actually get it on air I had doubts that it would ever happen. A string of TV executives, from the BBC and ITV as well as independent companies, told me that my stage show would make good television after watching the early West End performances in 1990. The problem we always came up against was that there was a general nervousness over hypnosis in the higher echelons of the television industry. I think they were terrified that viewers would be turned into zombies in their homes! There were other problems as well. Thames TV were on the verge of signing me up for a series when they suddenly lost their ITV franchise. Fortunately, Carlton TV, the company which took over, recognised the potential of the shows, asked me to join them and at last gave me the big beak I had waited so long for. I made my debut on their first major show, their New Years' Eve special in 1992 as one of their "faces for the future," along with a new band called Take That and up-and-coming comedian Frank Skinner. Four months later my TV show, the Hypnotic World Of Paul McKenna, was transmitted on the Easter Bank Holiday Monday. It had strong competition from Tom Cruise's movie

(left) With the gorgeous and talented Gloria Estefan.
(right) Wet Wet Wet were a massive hit when they came on the show.
(far right) The Bee Gees enjoyed themselves!

It is screened in these countries —

Australia
New Zealand
Denmark
Finland
The Netherlands
Norway
Sweden
South Africa
Hong Kong
India
Israel
Bahrain
Bangladesh
Burma
Cambodia
China
Cyprus
Egypt
Iran
Iraq
Jordan
Kuwait
Malaysia
Nepal
North and
South Korea
Oman
Palestine
Philippines
Saudi Arabia
Singapore
Syria
Slovenia
Thailand
Taiwan
Turkey
Vietnam
United
Arab Emirates
Mongolia
and Qatar
United States of
America.

Days Of Thunder on BBC1, but, to much amazement within the industry, the viewers were more interested in seeing hypnotised people than the Hollywood idol. We were all shocked that we pulled in 12 million viewers, at least 5 million more than Tom. I've made three series of Hypnotic World and various specials including Hypnotic Superstars, which, again to my surprise, have had international appeal, selling to 42 countries. It's even a hit in outer Mongolia – which I thought was a joke from our TV sales department until I saw the contract with the company there. People also watch it in countries such as China, Cambodia, Iran and Iraq – though I don't think I would want to count Saddam Hussein as a fan.

Strangely Belgian TV bought the shows but were forced to take them off the air – they were probably too funny for a country where humour is almost illegal.

In the first series ITV bosses, fearing that hypnosis alone would not keep viewers hooked for a whole 30 minutes, introduced musical guests. These included Wet Wet Wet, Gloria Estefan, Lulu, Chris Rea and the Bee Gees. However ITV were inundated with requests from viewers demanding more hypnotism – and so the musical acts struck their last note.

Now, the Bits you don't See on TV

As most of the routines on my TV show don't last for more than four minutes, I can quite understand why some people are staggered when I tell them just how many weeks of work and the number of people that go into putting just one of them together. Sometimes I can't help wondering myself why it takes so long!

For instance, preparation on routines for my August Bank Holiday Special 1995 – featuring the 10 best ever subjects – started six weeks before it was filmed. My manager Clare and I began by getting together with the seven programme associates who work permanently on the show to thrash out ideas in a small office in London's Covent Garden. It is where about half the routines begin their life, the rest are designed by Clare and myself. Coming up with a good hypnotic routine isn't like writing ordinary linear comedy, it's more like building a hologram. For that reason, our programme associates are not traditional writers, but people with a weird surreal way of looking at the world.

For eight hours, we chucked ideas for routines back and forth, dumping many because they were either too complicated or not funny enough. One of the definite winners was a sketch in which a subject, whose dream car is a Testarossa, is hypnotised to think a plastic kids' car is his gleaming red Ferrari. I explain it has no insurance, but allow the subject to take it for a spin – with tragic consequences. A hard-man character – we instantly thought of soccer star Vinny Jones – rams into the back of him in another plastic kids' car, but accuses the subject of reversing into him.

A policeman, who has arrived on a toy bike, takes Jones' side, pointing out: "How can I disbelieve such an upstanding member of the community?" Of course, we never know how a subject is going to react, but it's most likely he would by now be in a complete panic, remembering he has no insurance. Then the sketch finishes with the PC telling him that his vehicle must be removed – and a JCB digger rolls on and crushes it.

We all agreed the routine would be a hit. One of the production assistants immediately set about booking Vinny Jones and, for the policeman's role, TV presenter Ross King who had shown me how funny he could be when I hypnotised him on BBC1's Children In Need special in 1994. Both agreed immediately – Vinny was particularly keen because he had seen me in a stage show. Now we write their scripts and send them off to them. These are only ever outlines of what we believe might happen, because with hypnotised subjects you can never really tell until the night. The same is being done for all the other eight sketches on that show.

A week later the real work starts when everybody – the set designers, programme associates, producer, director, costume lady and props man as well as ten volunteers – arrive at the rehearsal rooms in Brixton, South London. We spend an exhausting day testing all the routines with the volunteers – they're imaginative subjects from my stage shows who are keen to be hypnotised again but they won't be used in the real TV show. We try out a routine, with different subjects, five or six times over the next fortnight to find ways of improving it, as every subject interprets it in their own individual way. Some have to be drastically re-worked, but the 'Vinny' sketch, as it has become known, is hilarious every time so is hardly altered.

THE DAY OF FILMING

10:00 I arrive, ready for a 12-hour day, at the London Television Studios on the South Bank of The Thames. We film in the largest studio No 1, seating 500 people, which is the home of many of ITV's biggest family shows including Barrymore, Blind Date and Surprise Surprise.

For most of the day, we are locked in rehearsals, estimating where we think the subjects will move, though we are not always right. Luckily our director, Martin Scott is never phased. We can not afford to run overtime because just a few minutes extra costs thousands of pounds. I rehearse all the routines with ten young actors and actresses standing in for the hypnotised subjects. Obviously I never use them on the real shows but I'm always intrigued by the way that the actors behave so differently from the people who are genuinely hypnotised. I take this to be positive proof that these routines could not be faked as sceptics have suggested.

15:30 The celebrities starring in the routines arrive to rehearse their roles. Also in the line-up for the show are Roy Barraclough (*Coronation Street*'s Alec Gilroy) and former *EastEnders* star Leslie Grantham. We had been a little nervous about Vinny, particularly because he's not an actor. But he turns out to be a pro – arriving on time, word perfect – while Ross *is* the part in his uniform.

Many stars who have appeared in the show have told me how fascinating they found it sharing the stage with "amateurs" because of their

unpredictability. On a lot of occasions the celebrities have found it hard to keep straight faces to some of the reactions of the subjects, especially as they so earnestly believe what they are saying.

During one routine, Gareth Hunt was playing a vicar conducting the marriage of a hypnotised couple. The bride was given a suggestion that she found the vicar very attractive, but after the cameras stopped rolling she carried on professing her undying love to him, with her arms wrapped tightly around his neck. He had to walk over to me with the young lady literally hanging from him to get me to wake her from the suggestion.

17:00 Martin Scott and I go through technical aspects, such as where to stand at particular times and which camera to talk to. Scene shifters are setting up the road scene for the Vinny sketch, complete with a T-junction and traffic lights. A JCB is also being manoeuvred into position behind a piece of scenery.

Meanwhile Vinny and Ross join the other stars in the make-up room, mainly to take the shine off their faces.

17:25 Break from rehearsal for dinner with the guests in the delightful canteen. I usually eat nothing more exotic than fish and chips with baked beans!

17:55 In my dressing room, I change from jeans and casual shirt into a suit. We have wardrobe assistants who work on our show, but Clare always has the final say on my ties. I also grab the chance to read my suggestions for the show for the final time.

18:00 Studio staff open the doors to the 500-strong audience, all over 18 years old because of television guidelines. Unlike many shows, we never advertise anywhere for our audience. They have all been found at our live shows, where they have filled in forms asking for tickets, which means that they know what to expect.

18:15 I put myself into trance for 15 minutes to prepare for the long evening ahead. I create images of the evening going really well, and the relaxation helps give me energy to get through the evening. To me, 15 minutes of hypnotic trance is equivalent to two hours of conventional sleep.

18:30 Off to the make up room. This wasn't something I had to face when working on radio!

18:35 Paul Alexander, the script editor, makes some last minute changes to my lines which are typed into the Autocue (electronic word prompter). Of course, we never have any idea what the subjects are going to say or how they will react during the show. So the opening link is the only bit of script for me.

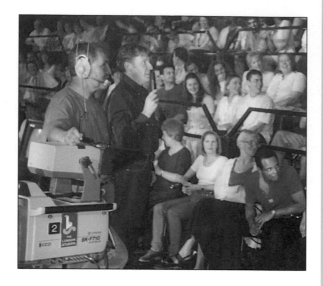

HYPNOTISING THE TV SUBJECTS

I know many viewers are fascinated by how I put the subjects into a trance, but we are not allowed under the TV rules to broadcast what I say during the induction. I believe that is with good reason because, otherwise, some people watching at home could be hypnotised. The last thing I want is granny leaping about like Elvis in the living room. There is one story, probably apocryphal, about a hypnotist sending thousands of viewers into a trance on Italian TV, then having to snap each one of them out of it for hours on the phone afterwards.

Before I ask for volunteers, I always stress that those who suffer from epilepsy, clinical depression, any psychiatric condition or are hyper-glyceamic, pregnant, or extremely stressed should not volunteer.

Here is a guide of how I put the subjects into trance. The only time I didn't follow this pattern was for the August Bank Holiday show in 1995 because we usually feature the best subjects from the previous series.

18:40 Top TV warm-up man Ray Turner cranks up the audience with some gags and get them used to laughing and applauding.

18:50 Dr Chris Pattinson, a respected medical doctor who uses hypnosis in treatment of his patients, takes his seat in the audience. He is hired by ITV as an independent observer at all the shows to see that everything is done exactly by the book.

18:55 Ray introduces me to give a preliminary talk where I explain a few simple studio rules, such as "If you see yourself on one of the monitors during the show, don't point and say 'Oh I'm on telly'".

19:00 The music starts, I walk out and do my first introduction to camera for real.

19:10 First I ask for volunteers. Around 60 people rush down to the stage from the audience. I have noticed the number has got greater, particularly at the stage shows, the longer the TV series has been going. At one time there used to be only about a dozen people wanting to take part.

19:20 Next I do a handclasp with the volunteers. I ask them to clasp their hands together and imagine that they are locked, bolted, glued, cemented together and that they cannot open their hands however hard they try. This is a

which disorientates them, then get them to fall backwards as I catch them and lay them on the ground. I then begin the induction for the rest of the volunteers, asking them to count backwards from 300 and systematically relax their bodies.

suggestibility test. It shows me which people are good at concentrating and have good imaginations, these are essential keys to a good subject for stage or TV hypnosis.

19:30 I sit some of the volunteers on chairs before carrying out "rapid inductions" on a couple of people. A rapid induction is a dramatic way of putting somebody into trance and acts as a powerful suggestion to the other people on stage.

19:35 During the rapid induction I stand next to the subject and ask them to close their eyes. I tip their head backwards,

19:45 All this time I am sorting out the people who are concentrating, looking for physiological signs of trance such as rapid eye movement and deep relaxation of the facial muscles. By the point at which I actually start giving the subjects small suggestions I probably have about thirty volunteers left. I do some small routines, asking them to carry out simple tasks using their imaginations. Clare, the producer and I watch them and discuss which subjects we think are the best. When we have agreed on the final ten volunteers I ask them, whilst hypnotised, to raise their hand if there is any reason why they should not take part in the show. If they all indicate that they are happy to continue we have our ten stars for the evening. Now I can relax for five minutes as I wake the subjects up to be fitted with radio microphones.

This particular show was an hour long, but a half hour show takes almost as long to film. About 45 minutes of this is the induction where we choose the ten volunteers. The actual routines are fairly quick to film but there are so many changes to the set, lighting and cameras that the evening

49

takes a lot out of everyone involved, probably with the exception of the subjects who tend to think they have only been there ten minutes. It often feels more like ten hours to me and the crew.

Sometimes routines don't work out exactly as planned. One subject called Billy was given the suggestion that the glove puppet on his hand was insulting him. He started to argue with it before punching it to the ground. He was rolling about on the floor thumping the puppet and at one point the cameraman was laughing so hard he collapsed. I quickly jumped in and woke the subject. We were laughing for days as was Billy when he saw the video of himself.

Another time I gave a young lady a suggestion that she was cementing the studio floor and she was to get very irate at anybody who walked on it. We had to stop the filming for a technical reason and the producer wandered on to the set. She went crazy, screaming and shouting at him to "get off my wet cement" as she manhandled him on to an area that she apparently hadn't done yet. The poor producer looked to me for help, but I was too busy laughing.

He got his revenge when I gave two men the suggestion that I was the American President and they were my burly bodyguards. At one point the producer let off a loud bang which they thought

THE FINAL SKETCH: I've backed into him ...

was a gun shot. Hurling me to the ground, the two men threw themselves on top of me "for my protection". I couldn't even move or speak to tell them to "sleep".

20:00 Tony, Clare, and I take a break to discuss the filming.

20:30 At last it's time to put the Vinny routine into operation. Will all those weeks of planning pay off? Fortunately the subject is superb. He is horrified when PC King sides with Vinny, guilt-ridden when he suddenly remembers he has no insurance and just mortified when the JCB crushes his "dream" car, throwing his arms in the air, shaking his head and shouting "no". The audience are in hysterics.

22:00 It's the end of the evening I wake everybody up and make sure they are all back to normal.

22:30 I join Vinny, Ross and the other celebrities and subjects who have taken part for a well-earned drink together in the hospitality suite behind the studio.

A couple of days later we get all ten volunteers back to a smaller studio and show them the footage of what they did, film their reactions and ask them what they remember and what they felt. We then cut their reactions into the show, edit, add music and you see the finished product on your screens a few weeks later. This show is first screened in Britain but then shown in forty-two other countries to over 200 million people!

... the Old Bill arrives ...

... and it's me they arrest !

My Top TV Routines

Time and again I am asked to name the funniest thing that ever happened during my TV shows. I've always been stumped for an answer because it's impossible to choose just one routine out of more than 200. But, after watching hours of videos, I've selected some of my all-time favourites. What makes them successful, of course, isn't the ideas behind the routines, but the lively imagination of the subjects taking part. Rarely can I, or, I suspect, the viewers, predict what they are going to say or even do next. As for the celebrity guests, I only have the utmost respect for them for entering into the spirit of the show – and allowing themselves to be constantly upstaged by the subjects with such good grace. The one thing that is clear from any of the routines is that the stars of my shows are definitely the subjects.

BLIND DATE

What man would turn down a date with lovely model Linda Lusardi? Three of my subjects were hypnotised to be adamant that it was the last thing they wanted in a spoof Blind Date sketch. At all costs they had to make sure she didn't pick them to be her Blind Date. They certainly tried hard:

Linda: I'm a bit of a daddy's girl. If I took you home to meet my father what would you do to impress him?

No 1: I would tell him how dreadful looking he was to start with.

No 2: I would leave you there.

No 3: I would take him a bunch of bananas.

Linda: I love animals. What animal would you compare yourself with and why?

No 1: A tortoise because I'm slow and lethargic and I moan like Victor Meldrew.

No 2 : A swordfish because I'm sharp and nasty.

No 3: A greyhound because if you pick me tonight I'm off and running.

Linda: If you choose me tonight where will you take

me on our dream date?

No 1: Down the dogs.

No 2: I would take you back to your dad, as I said.

No 3: I would take you down to the London Dungeon where you wouldn't look out of place.

After much deliberating, Linda picks No 3 but when he sees her, he says: "Whenever I watch the show they always have nice women on!"

NEWS AT TEN

Under hypnosis, a subject, Paul, happily answered my probing questions about his life, where he lived, his car etc, without realising it. Then he found himself co-presenting a spoof News at Ten with Angela Rippon. What he didn't know was that his earlier answers had been inserted into her news items. His reactions as she read the news – all about him – were hilarious…

Angela: Good evening, I'm Angela Rippon. Police are this evening trying to track down an assembly process worker called Paul whose three bedroom house in Tudor Crescent today fell into a 50ft hole. Paul is in line for half a million pounds compensation, but only if he can be traced within the next five minutes.

Paul(*Looks shocked but carries on trying to read the news*): More news now and Prince Charles is to marry again.

Angela: The Prince's new bride, Hazel from Portsmouth,…

Paul: Hang on, that's my wife!

Angela (*continues patiently*) … is a government worker. They have been seeing each other in secret for some time. Hazel says the Prince is the first real man she has been out with after a sad succession of wimps, drunks and morons. Hazel will also become the first Queen to have modelled nude when her *Playboy* centrefold hits the newsstands tomorrow.

Paul (*increasingly bewildered and stuttering*): You shouldn't be saying this on air.

Angela: And now Paul with the weather.

Paul: It started off bad and it's getting worse!

Angela: … And finally a runaway steam roller ploughed into a parked car this evening. The car, a blue Rover 216, (*reads out his registration number*), was completely flattened …

Paul (*now very angry and shouting*): No, no, no!

Angela (*straight-faced*): Insurers who say this type of accident isn't covered are still trying to trace the owner of the vehicle, so they can slip it under his door.

Paul: That's unbelievable. I've lost my house, my car and my wife. It's all gone.

Angela (*helpfully*): You might be able to get the furniture back, I should think …

Leslie Grantham, who, of course, made his name as Dirty Den in *EastEnders*, starred as a very convincing police superintendent who had taken one of his young up-and-coming PCs out for dinner at a posh restaurant. He was keen to give him promotion. The only trouble was that I had hypnotised the PC's wife, played by Liza, to be a bit common. I told her she was not going to be something she's not and always speaks her mind. She would grow more determined to prove this the more she drank (though she was actually only sipping a glass of water) …

Grantham (*as police superintendent*): Would you like a drink?

Liza: Yeah, I wouldn't mind some of the old plonk. Thanks very much geezer. Cheers big ears.

Grantham: What do you normally eat when you go out?

Liza: Fish and chips.

Andrew (*PC*): Only ever on a Friday. Fish and chips on a Friday.

Liza (*holding up utensil for eating snails*): Excuse me, are these for doing yer eyelashes with?

Grantham: As you know this restaurant serves nouvelle cuisine. Do you like that?

Liza: Nouvelle what? Nouvelle cuisine, that's when you go to MFI, innit, and you order a new kitchen?

Grantham: As you know, your husband is up for promotion to Sergeant. Do you think you can cope with that?

Liza (*increasingly drunk*): These blokes came round the house with this big bag and it looked like talcum powder.

Andrew: It was talcum powder.

Liza: It was the dearest talcum powder I've ever seen. He was flogging it for 20 quid and there was only a tiny bit in the bag.

Andrew: It was from Selfridges.

Liza: And I'd like to thank you very much, Superintendent, for allowing my husband to use the car for off duty taxi-ing. The money comes in very handy.

Grantham: What do you think are your husband's best qualities?

Liza: Well, those horses and the dope pedalling he did.

Grantham: Well taking all the evidence into account, I'd just like to say you've got the job.

MISS HYPNOTIC WORLD

GORGEOUS TV presenter Debbie Greenwood helped me when we judged the finalists for my Miss World contest. Mind you, competition wasn't tough; the other subjects believed that the top prize was a night out with Jeremy Beadle, so they didn't try too hard, leaving the floor open for the lucky winner!

TV CRITICS

It got me a ticking off from TV watchdogs, the Independent Television Commission – they thought some of the language was too suggestive – but one of my favourite sketches is still the TV Critics. Three subjects were shown a clip from the children's TV series *Trumpton* of firemen lifting up a ladder to get a rocking horse out of a tree. Quite innocuous, you would have thought, only I had hypnotised David to think he was a pompous critic who believes that what he saw was the finest piece of TV ever and Mandy was a watchdog who was always complaining about disgusting TV. Only Paul was down to earth and saw it for what it was. All thought they were right when they debated the clip on a pretentious late-night arts show which I presented:

Me: Well, if I can turn to you first David for your initial impressions of that clip.

David (*pompous critic*): Well, Barry, your name is Barry, isn't it? I thought it was absolutely wonderful. You've uncovered a beautiful gem – such vivid colour. The costumes were marvellous, the storylines you could compare to Henry V – or Much Ado About Nothing. Oh, it was perfect, don't you agree?

WHAT THE SUBJECT SAID: Graham on believing he had won the Miss Hypnotic World title for Austria: "It was so important to win because it was for my country as far as I could see. I remember being really nervous about the situation. I had to get out there and win"

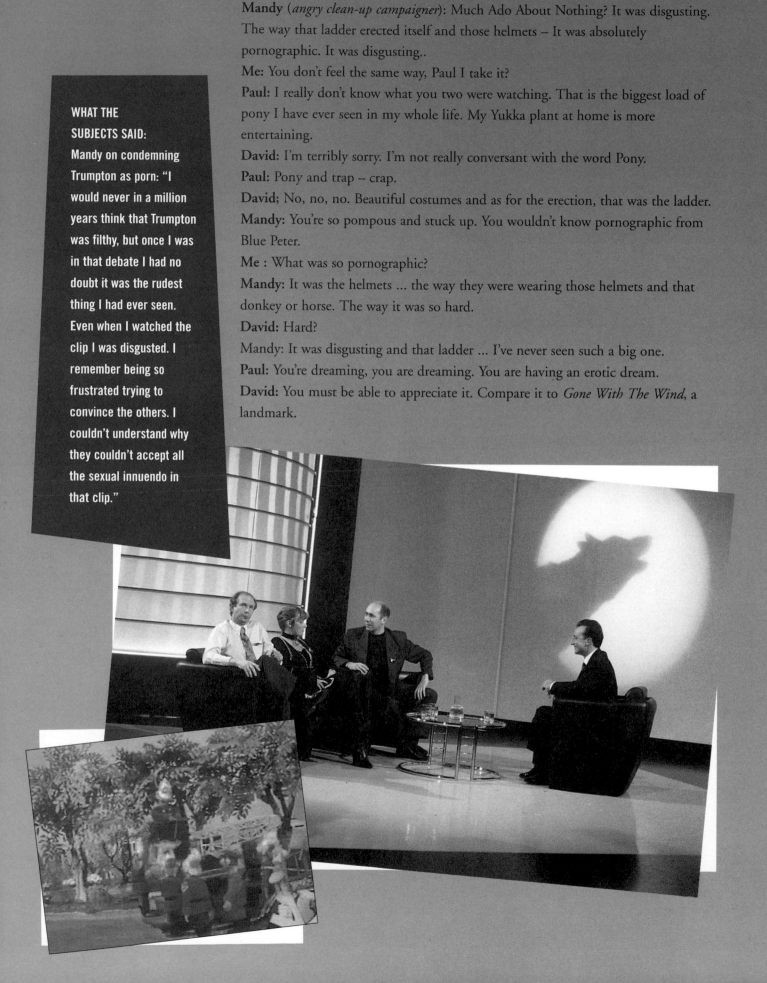

Mandy (*angry clean-up campaigner*): Much Ado About Nothing? It was disgusting. The way that ladder erected itself and those helmets – It was absolutely pornographic. It was disgusting..

Me: You don't feel the same way, Paul I take it?

Paul: I really don't know what you two were watching. That is the biggest load of pony I have ever seen in my whole life. My Yukka plant at home is more entertaining.

David: I'm terribly sorry. I'm not really conversant with the word Pony.

Paul: Pony and trap – crap.

David; No, no, no. Beautiful costumes and as for the erection, that was the ladder.

Mandy: You're so pompous and stuck up. You wouldn't know pornographic from Blue Peter.

Me : What was so pornographic?

Mandy: It was the helmets ... the way they were wearing those helmets and that donkey or horse. The way it was so hard.

David: Hard?

Mandy: It was disgusting and that ladder ... I've never seen such a big one.

Paul: You're dreaming, you are dreaming. You are having an erotic dream.

David: You must be able to appreciate it. Compare it to *Gone With The Wind*, a landmark.

Paul: My farts are more entertaining than that.

David; In that case we are all grateful we don't spend any time in your bathroom.

Paul: I've got a Jacuzzi.

David: That figures.

Me: So in conclusion, could you sum up the piece you have seen in a word or sentence.

David: Oscar-winning.

Mandy: Hard porn.

Paul: I just haven't got the words to describe such utter nonsense.

WORK – OUT NIGHTMARE

Even in her worst nightmare, superfit Michaela Strachen can't have thought she would have to work with a keep-fit class as hopeless as that in our routine. She was supposed to be making a work-out video, but Jane Fonda it certainly wasn't.

One of her class, Steve, had been hypnotised to think he was so lazy he even tried to go to sleep when she suggested simply lifting a finger. Worse still another subject, Jay, had been hypnotised to moan that all her exercises were extremely dangerous – even when she asked them to jump up and down.

Jay immediately protested: "That is extremely dangerous. You must have all heard what happened to Zebedee."

STITCHED UP AGAIN

Anyone who becomes well-known has to put up with things that are completely untrue being written about them from time to time. Humour is a good way to redress the balance so I hypnotised some subjects to believe that they all had an outrageous story about someone who had been hypnotised by me. I played the sleaze-hungry editor of a Sunday tabloid – eager to reward the person with the most outlandish tale with a fistful of bank notes.

Me: We really want to stitch this McKenna geezer up. So who wants to go first then?

Mark: Right, my mate is under the lights and McKenna is going on about how hot it is. He says it's like you're on the beach, but it's hotter than that, really hot and you are burning up. And this is going to sound stupid, but now my mate reckons he is a hotdog. He has given up his job so he can go down to Tottenham Court Road Station every day and stand next to the guy who is there sizzling sausages and beg him to cover him in ketchup. He says he won't be happy until he can lie in a great big bun and be covered in ketchup.

Arabella: Well, I know this girl, who works in my office, who was hypnotised by McKenna. She is 26, really pretty and she now thinks she's a man.

Samantha: Another friend of mine went on that show and she was told she was a carpet. And now everytime you go round her house she just lies down on the floor in front of you and wants you to walk all over her.

Mark: This guy I know reckons he's a pilchard now. He covers himself in ketchup and hangs around fish stalls and tries to slide onto the ice when no-one is looking.

Samantha: Maybe it's the Ketchup thing.

ONE WEDDING, ONE BRIDE AND TWO GROOMS

Gareth Hunt, the brilliant actor, played a vicar with hysterical results. A subject, Delia, was hypnotised to believe she was the bride, but she suddenly found herself at the altar with an overwhelming crush on the vicar. Martin was the groom who wants the day to run smoothly. Meanwhile subjects in the congregation are hypnotised to come up with bizarre and unusual reasons for why the happy couple shouldn't marry.

Gareth: Dearly beloved we are gathered here today to join this man and this woman in Holy Matrimony. Marriage is a holy estate not to be entered into lightly so think carefully before you commit your bodies to each other.

Martin(*noticing Delia smiling and waving at the vicar*): What do you think you're doing?

Gareth: Please try to concentrate Martin, it is your wedding after all. Now does anyone here present know any reason why these two lovely people should not be brought together in holy wedlock?

Yes, madam, you have something to say?

CM 1(*Congregation member*): He is already married to my mum!

Gareth: Please please!

CM2: I don't think her other five husbands are going to be pleased.

CM3: I was only knocking her off last night.

Gareth: I could be knocking you off if you carry on like that.

CM1: She's not real. She's an alien.

Martin: Does she not look real to you?

CM1: Her face, her face, pull her face.

Gareth: Do either of you know of any reason why you should not be married?

Martin: No.

Delia (*Still smiling at the vicar*): No.

Gareth: Do you take this woman to be your lawful wedded wife? Who's got the ring?

Chaos breaks out as they fight over the ring and the bride ends up dragging Gareth away with her.

DEGENERATION GAME

Mimic Bobby Davro was hilarious as Bruce Forsyth when he hosted our spoof of *The Generation Game*, called The Degeneration Game. Joseph had been hypnotised to believe everything on the conveyer belt is his. The 'contestants' had been hypnotised to not understand how to do the games. In one of them, they had to copy my skill at putting on a pair of trousers. One of the subjects ended up putting them on their head.

Bobby: Do you recognise any of this?

Joseph: Wait wait this is mine. It's all mine. This is my lampshade. Where do you get them from? I'd recognise this mop and bucket anywhere. Right, I will call the police. Is there a policeman in the audience?

Joseph tries to pull the goods off the belt; a fight breaks out. Bobby pulls them off him as Joseph shouts for someone to get the police.

BRAINBUSTERS

After his success in hosting *Blockbusters*, Bob Holness got the chance to front another very similar show called Brainbusters. It would have gone smoothly if John had not been hypnotised to think that the number 7 was missing from his memory.

Bob: Good evening and welcome. John is our first contestant and you're an engineer, is that right?

John: Yes.

Bob: How many wonders of the World are there?

John: Eight.

(And to every question all he could say was eight...)

Bob: How many days of the week? Complete this well known title, Snow White and the ... dwarfs? Ian Fleming's famous spy was code-named 00 what? In the hit musical how many brides were there for how many brothers? Will you complete this film title The Magnificent ...?

John: Eight!

HYPNO MAN

In one of my most dramatic routines, I peeled off my shirt and revealed to one startled hypnotised volunteer that I was in fact the superhero 'Hypno-Man'. While he was in a trance, we were both strapped into harnesses with wires. I woke him up and – to his astonishment – taught him how to fly. I eventually got him flapping his arms and chanting "I believe in fairies" as he was raised up into the air.

CHILDREN IN NEED

Frank Bruno stole the show when I hypnotised him on the BBC1's *Children In Need Show* in 1994. He joined a celebrity line up of excellent subjects including Tony Blackburn, Faith Brown, Ross King, *GMTV*'s Amanda Reddington, *Watchdog*'s Simon Walton and *The Sun*'s Garry Bushell. Frank had everyone in hysterics when he joined Ross on my spoof chat show with a twist – both of them had been hypnotised to tell the biggest whoppers they could:

Me: Hello, good evening and welcome. Let's find out who our special guests are tonight. *(Turning to Ross)* And your name is?

Ross: Claudia Schiffer.

Me: The famous model. I didn't recognise you – you look a little different in real life. Do you do any other jobs?

Ross: I work in Tescos as well.

Me: Oh, what's on special offer at the moment?

Ross: Cornflakes at 74 pence.

Me (*turning to Frank*): What's your name by the way?

Frank: President Tutu.

Me: Such an honour to have you on the show. Are you President full-time or do you have another job?

Frank: Ducking and diving, selling cars.

Me: What happened to you on your way here?

Frank: I tripped over my wallet in Oxford Street.

Me (*turning to Ross*): Anything interesting you've been doing tonight Claudia?

Ross: I went to a club with Princess Diana to play strip poker.

CONTROL STRESS

Stress is caused by your body preparing to face a physical threat – and then doing nothing. When we get wound up our bodies prepare to hit something or to run away- that's how our ancestors stayed alive before man built towns with walls and weapons to defend himself.

Of course, nowadays, most of the problems and threats we face are psychological. We worry about exams, or money or what someone might say but our bodies still react physically. The body releases adrenaline into the bloodstream, digestion is halted, and blood is concentrated in the major muscles because the nervous system doesn't differentiate between a threat to your ego and a threat to your physical self. My six point plan helps you overcome stress and keep calm.

MY SIX POINT PLAN TO CONTROL STRESS

1 Breathe out deeply three times. If you feel yourself getting stressed, breathe out, all the way to the bottom of your lungs, then let go. The in breath happens automatically as your diaphragm pulls in more air. As you breathe all the way out you move your breathing from short, shallow breathing at the top of your lungs which is associated with stress, to deep long natural breaths from your diaphragm which sends a powerful signal to your body to calm down.

2 Be polite to yourself. A major cause of stress is internal dialogue – the way we talk to ourselves when we are thinking things through. Remember what sort of voice you used in your imagination last time you were stressed. And change the tone of the voice. If it was harsh, make it friendly, if it was high-pitched make it low, if it was fast slow it down. Change it in as many ways you want until it is more polite. You may still have to think things through, but you don't have to be rude to yourself!

3 Make one positive change to your environment every day. Research has shown that the more people express themselves in their surroundings the more relaxed they become – so every day do something, no matter how small to make your environment nicer. It could by picking a bunch of flowers for the kitchen or bringing a postcard in to work, it doesn't matter. just everyday do something to make your environment nicer for you.

4 Exercise every day. Stress has a large physical component – and one of the very best ways to relax is to use up that physical energy and preparation. Just twenty minutes in the gym or even a brisk walk for 15 minutes in the fresh air will help your body relax. It's so simple it's easy to forget, but exercise really is one of the best ways to get your mind and body balanced.

5 Reframe your situation. Our reactions are caused by how we interpret the world – nothing in itself is stressful, only the way we see it. If you see a person, a situation or an event as threatening, your body will register stress. So whenever something stresses, you see it in your mind's eye. Then drain out the colour, make the picture black and white – then imagine it shrinking, spinning away from you and disappearing. Any time you feel threatened do that again and then create a picture, in big, bold colour, of you dealing brilliantly with the situation.

6 Twice a day take a power nap. Your body has a natural tendency to relax every 90 minutes. You'll recognise these times by a sweet soft feeling in your muscles, your eyes want to close and it's difficult to concentrate. It doesn't matter if you ignore most of these times, but it is very good for

you to hitch a ride on them twice a day for five minutes or so. You wake up feeling refreshed and relaxed and you perform better. What's more, while you rested, your body's immune and healing system used the time to optimise your health.

So twice a day when you're feel a bit drowsy, take a power nap for just five minutes or so and you'll feel great and stay healthy.

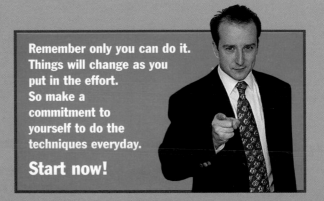

Remember only you can do it. Things will change as you put in the effort. So make a commitment to yourself to do the techniques everyday.

Start now!

THE STORY OF HYPNOTISM

STORY: MICK KIDD

ART: CHRIS GARRATT

FROM TIME IMMEMORIAL, HUMANKIND HAS ENTERED **TRANCE STATES**, WHETHER VIA **MEDITATION**—

YES — THE UNIVERSE IS NOT SUCH A BAD OLD PLACE WHEN YOU'VE REACHED NIRVANA LIKE MYSELF.

—OR 16 PINTS OF LAGER...

I'M ABOUT TO HAVE A PEAK EXPERIENCE.

HOLD EVERYTHING, —I'LL GET A BUCKET.

HYPNOTISM ITSELF WAS KNOWN TO **HIPPOCRATES** IN ANCIENT GREECE...

THAT'S RIGHT! —MATTER O'FACT, MY FRIENDS CALL ME **HYPNOCRATES**!

FATHER OF MEDICINE

...BUT IT WASN'T TILL THE **18TH CENTURY** THAT SCIENCE SOUGHT AN EXPLANATION...

HOW DOES HE **DO** THAT, DES?

ANIMAL MAGNETISM, HE SAYS.

I WILL INDUCE A HUGE CONVULSION, AFTER WHICH YOU'LL FEEL FANTASTIC.

I BET HE SAYS THAT TO ALL THE GALS.

TONITE! THE ONE AND ONLY ★ FRANZ **MESMER**

FATHER OF DES LYNHAM

MESMER WORKED WITH ALL THE BIG NAMES—

IT'S NO GOOD, DOC — —MY MIND'S A COMPLETE BLANK.

BLANK!

BEFORE

—WITH NOTABLE SUCCESS...

COSE FAN TUTTI FRUTTI

CONGRATULATIONS, MOZART — YOU'VE JUST INVENTED ROCK'N'ROLL!

AFTER

LATER CAME THE **MARQUIS DE PUYSEGUR**, WHO HYPNOTISED THE PEASANTS...

....WHEN I SNAP MY FINGERS YOU WILL ORGANISE THE FRENCH REVOLUTION....

OUI! OUI! 10-4!

JAMES BRAID IN ENGLAND...

GULP! HYPNOSIS AS ANAESTHETIC... ARE YOU SURE ABOUT THIS, DOC?

NO-BUT THERE'S ONLY ONE WAY TO FIND OUT...

...AND, IN AUSTRIA, **SIGMUND FREUD**...

HMM...SEEMS TO BE A SPOT OF ROLE REVERSAL HERE...

GRADUALLY, HYPNOTISM GAINED PROFESSIONAL RESPECTABILITY...

IT'S INCREDIBLE! —BUT IT WORKS!

Induce HYPNOSIS with HYPNO-EYES

"The best hypnotic instrument ever devised," says professional. New sensational hypnotic chart makes hypnotism easy and simple to master in just a few short hours. People will envy and respect your astonishing ability to control command. Be a...

How To Get Girls Through Hypnotism!

We Dare You To Try It!

Give Us 5 Days — And We'll Give You A New Modernized Method of Getting Girls Like Nothing You've Ever Seen Before — Let Us Prove It!

HOW TO HYPNOTIZE

IT'S EASY TO HYPNOTIZE... *when you know how!*

.....IN **U.F.O.** RESEARCH...

...IT WAS A ONE-EYED, ONE-HORNED FLYING PURPLE PEOPLE-EATER...

YAWN: DID IT HAVE ANY-ER-SPECIAL MESSAGE FOR MANKIND?

BEEP!

...IN FARMING...

...YOU WILL LAY MORE EGGS...YOU WILL LAY MORE EGGS...

ACTUALLY I'M A COCKEREL.

...AND OF COURSE IN SHOWBIZ...

WHAT I'D REALLY LIKE TO BE IS A ZEN MASTER.

THE END

My Story of Hypnotism

The idea of using hypnotic techniques goes back at least to the time of the ancient Greeks and Egyptians, indeed Hypnos is the Greek word for sleep. We find references to the use of hypnotic like techniques and procedures in The Hindu Vedas written about 1500 BC.

The growth of modern hypnosis began in the eighteenth century when Franz Anton Mesmer began practising as a doctor and became interested in the idea of magnetism as a cure. Mesmer set up a clinic in Paris which used baths of "magnetised" water and a very theatrical atmosphere to exploit the trance state.

Mesmer could therefore be credited with combining show business with hypnosis, as well as probably starting all the controversy (he was subsequently denounced by a Royal Commission as a charlatan). He said at the time "I am accused of being a common cheat, and those who believe in me are taunted with being fools. Such is apt to be the fate of new truths."

The first British pioneer of the subject was John Elliotson, a professor who championed the cause of mesmerism but was forced to resign. Nevertheless he continued to demonstrate the phenomena, leading to an increase in literature on the subject. In the nineteenth century the English surgeon James Braid first used the terms 'hypnotism', 'hypnotist' and 'hypnotic' in his book *Neurypnology* published in 1841. Braid pioneered the use of hypnosis as an alternative to anaesthetic drugs, a fascinating area which I have covered in *The Power of Hypnosis* on page 76.

Jean Martin Charcot, a Paris neurologist, found that hysterical symptoms such as paralysis, deafness and blindness could be brought on and taken away by hypnosis and his interest helped increase its acceptance by the medical profession.

More recently Milton Erickson has probably been the most influential person using hypnosis for therapy in this century and I consider Richard Bandler, a student of Erickson's, to be currently the leading expert in the subject today.

Things you never

knew

about

hypnosis

Nurses at the University of Manchester are now taught hypnosis as part of their training.

People can be hypnotised so that even the tendon reflex (making the leg jump when tapped on the knee) is eliminated.

In hypnotic trance, the heart beat can be made faster or slower and the amount of blood circulating in any limb can be increased.

Jackie Kennedy-Onassis used hypnotherapy to "relive and let go of" some tragic events in her life.

Stomach contractions caused by hunger can be eliminated if a person is hypnotised with the suggestion of eating a large meal.

Short sighted people can be hypnotised to change the shape of their eyeballs and improve their distance vision for a short time.

Suggestion can cause the body to produce a violent burn where nothing has touched the skin.

Svengali, a character in George Du Maurier's novel Trilby, is the prototype of the evil, sinister and manipulative hypnotist.

Kevin Costner flew his personal hypnotist to Hawaii to cure his seasickness during the filming of Waterworld.

Hypnosis is very effective in the treatment of eczema, psoriasis and irritable bowel syndrome.

Accounts of what we would now call Hypnosis can be found in the Bible and the Talmud.

Dentists are now widely using hypnosis as a safe alternative to anaesthetic.

The Wall Street Hypnosis Center treats victims of "trading disorder" using hypnotherapy.

Sporting Champions: Psyched Up to Win

As a child I was not massively interested in sport, except for football, but, now I find myself working more often with international sports men and women than with people from any other walk of life. Perhaps the intense competition that modern sport stars face means they demand complete psychological as well physical fitness.

I do my best to help sportsmen from every field achieve their absolute maximum. Some of those who have publicly talked about consulting me include WBC World heavyweight champion Frank Bruno, Olympic swimmer Adrian Moorhouse, Wimbledon champion Pat Cash, WBC Super Middleweight Champion Nigel Benn, Premier League soccer stars Chris Armstrong and Iain Dowie, England cricketer Robin Smith and British pole vault champion Kate Staples (alias Gladiators star Zodiac).

The results have been record-breaking. Hypnotherapy has helped Adrian clip two seconds off his personal best, Kate has actually broken the British record 25 times and Robin Smith returned to playing cricket for England more confident than he'd ever been. He was the top scorer in the 2nd and 3rd 1995 Test Matches against the West Indies. I was touched when Frank Bruno revealed how I had helped him with positive thinking after he won the heavyweight WBC championship in September 1995, but I always say that really the victories belong entirely to the athletes.

(left) A victorious
Nigel Benn.
(right) A delighted Iain
Dowie.

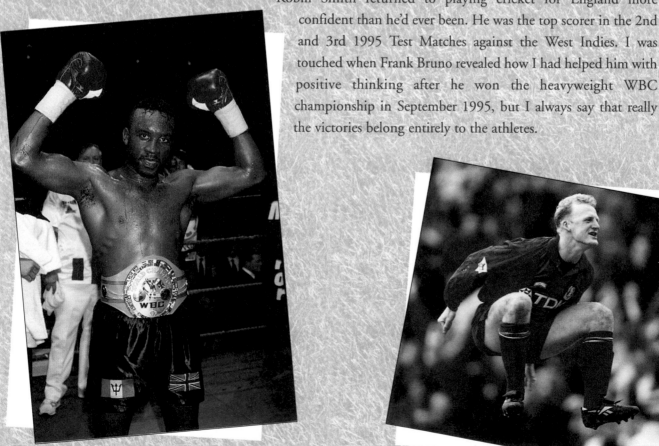

Hypnosis is very different, and much more effective, than many types of traditional Sports psychology. A lot of athletes practise mental rehearsal, but don't realise the importance of the way they should picture success. For example, if you imagine yourself winning a race, is it appealing? You can do a lot to improve that picture – turn the colour up, the brightness up, make it twice as big. Doing these things increases the feelings and can add to the intensity of the result.

When working with sports people, I get them to go back in their minds and review all the times they have played at peak performance. Their unconscious mind notes the various components, of those peak experiences from the amount of blood pressure in their little finger to the amount of muscular tension in, say, their right leg. We then build all of those moments of excellence into a super state of mind and body which they can trigger whenever they want too.

An example of this is the work I've done with Kate Staples. She feels it really helped her and amazingly we can now do this over the phone just minutes before she is about to jump, wherever she is in the world. She also listens to motivational tapes and inspirational music during the competitions.

Essentially I change an athlete's self image and I get them to see themselves as a champion so they unconsciously communicate this to their opponent from the start. I did a lot of work with British Olympic fencer Johnny Davis. One of the things I noticed was that he didn't enter the arena very confidently at competitions. So we worked on that until he did. He said his performance had improved out of all recognition, ensuring he had the best Olympics of his career, competing for the English team in Barcelona in 1992.

Another technique that I find really effective for sports people is 'slow time'. You've probably had the experience of queuing in the bank for a few minutes, but it seems like ages. Time hasn't slowed down, but your perception of time has. I simply teach some sports people to slow down time in their mind so they can move faster in the real world. That way they have more time to anticipate their opponent, hit the

Frank Bruno with me after his successful challenge for the WBC Heavyweight title. (left) At his home and (right) congratulating him just minutes after the fight.

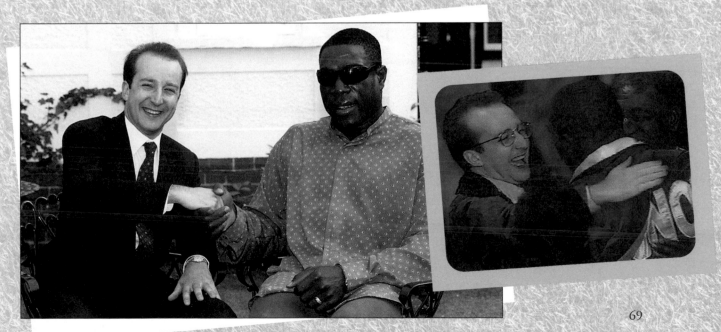

ball, or just make a decision. The racing driver Jackie Stewart once said that he only ever drove fast twice in his life and both times it scared him.

I encourage people to practise playing 100 games in their mind in an afternoon winning every one of them – it makes you feel like a champion and you start to play like one in reality.

When I first showed up to work with Crystal Palace football team, I got them to play these imaginary games. They must have thought I was crazy – I think a couple of players even thought it was some sort of voodoo and I was going to start sacrificing chickens! After I explained it was a motivational technique, they really got into the spirit of tackling imaginary defenders and scoring every time – something they hadn't been used to. We played five games in an afternoon and in their minds they won every single one.

I could see that the main body of work was going to be in getting them to change their belief in themselves, to boost their confidence as a team. They were very demoralised. One of the players, Iain Dowie, responded particularly well – and incredibly his goal scoring went through the roof. For the short period of time I worked with them I definitely noticed they became much more focused and were working better as a team. I only wish I had started working with them earlier in the season.

(left) Robin Smith.
(right) Chris Armstrong.

Of course, at the end of the day, Hypnosis is no substitute for discipline, dedication and tough training in all areas. All hypnosis can do is help any sportsman achieve his very best. It can help put somebody into the best state of mind for an event and if you add this to the best state of body it is an overpowering combination.

When Nigel Benn thanked me publicly after retaining his title in the Gerald McLellan fight, at least one newspaper accused me of hypnotising him to "be a terror". Such nonsense is laughable. Nigel came to me because he had some emotional issues on his mind. We

worked on those and then he was able to focus more effectively on his training and the fight so it was only indirectly that I helped his boxing.

Of course it doesn't go down well with everyone. Chris Eubank called for an inquiry into the use of hypnosis in boxing after losing his title to Steve Collins, who had admitted a hypnotist had helped him in the run up to the fight. Eubank called hypnosis legal cheating, but the governing board of boxing thought differently and after an investigation they gave it the green light.

Ireland's football manager Jackie Charlton, who appeared alongside me on a TV debate, heard me explain that what I do with my sporting clients is to talk to them, motivate them, get them to imagine things in a relaxed state of mind. He said it sounded just like what he did with his team during his pep talks except that he didn't call it hypnosis. He was right and the reason most people criticise hypnosis is because they just don't understand this.

Every single athlete in the world has to imagine what they are going to do. And, in some respects, all coaches are intuitive hypnotists who give suggestions in the form of encouragement and motivation. A powerful suggestion delivered well can definitely induce greater speed and flexibility. I know people who can override pain, for example, simply by virtue of their military training. They don't need to be hypnotised to bring about the same results of natural anaesthetic. So few people realise that hypnosis is essentially just talking to someone and getting them to use their imagination. At the end of the day it is all just words and imagination.

(left) Adrian Moorhouse.
(right) Pat Cash.

MY SIX POINT PLAN TO BE A WINNER

This plan for success in sport can be used by both amateurs and professionals:

1 WATCH a number of good performances by your personal sports hero.

2 RELAX and close your eyes.

3 PICTURE your hero performing in the way you admire most. Build up the image as richly as you can adding details including sounds and feelings.

4 IMAGINE asking your hero for help. Walk up behind your hero and step inside his or her body, putting it on almost like a suit. See with their eyes, hear with their ears, feel what they feel.

5 EXPLORE what it is like to be in your hero's world. Discover answers to questions which have been puzzling you.

6 STEP back out of your hero, thanking him or her for their help. Return to waking consciousness, bringing with you what you have learned.

Remember only you can do it. Things will change as you put in the effort. So make a commitment to yourself to do the techniques everyday.

Start now!

Trick vs Trance
the Big Controversy

Since my show has been on television, I've been constantly shocked and bemused by the amount of nonsense written on hypnosis. It would be funny, except that the misinformation hurts a number of people and gives a distorted and dangerous view of the subject.

When I first began, the press mainly refused to believe hypnosis even existed and whenever my shows were reviewed the main criticism was that they were unbelievable. Eventually it got so bad that I had to put the record straight and in 1994, I actually took legal proceedings against the BBC and Terry Wogan for claiming my show was fixed. I took the action reluctantly, but I felt I had no choice because if I didn't make my point it would become accepted that he was right.

At first, the BBC actually tried to fight the case, even going to the lengths of interviewing subjects from my show to ask them if they were really hypnotised or just acting. Eventually they realised that it was all genuine and ended up paying my legal costs and damages. The *Sun's* cartoonist, Tom Johnston, saw it this way at the time (see below).

"SO YOU MET PAUL McKENNA AND YOU STILL THINK HE'S A FAKE!"

Terry and I settled the matter amicably and made up at The Children In Need TV show in 1994. Terry joked with me on the show: "As you know, Paul I am as sceptical as the next man." After he chatted to the line up of celebrities I had hypnotised on the show, including Frank Bruno, he turned to me, laughed and said: "I hate to say you may well have convinced me."

Next the media attacked the shows from a moral standpoint, branding them humiliating and degrading to the people involved. In all the years I have been performing I have never received one letter of complaint and nobody has ever come to me after a show and told me that they felt in any way embarrassed by what they did. In fact people are always saying how they love taking part. They are the stars, they really enjoy letting their hair down and effectively forgetting their responsibilities for a night. Some people come on stage several times because they enjoy the experience so much and I have to be very vigilant to try not to use the same people twice so others can have a go.

More recently stage hypnosis even became the subject of a debate in parliament. Essentially, I believe there are three main questions to answer:

Is stage hypnosis dangerous?

Hypnosis has been blamed for headaches, nausea, increased nervousness, and all sorts of other more bizarre neurotic manifestations.

What is particularly amusing about the entire question of hypnosis and its dangers is that only those who consider hypnosis to be some sort of altered state ever raise the issue. If we phrase it properly : *Is there anything dangerous about an individual relaxing, using his imagination, and following along with suggestions* - the answer is a resounding NO!

I have spoken at length with Dr Graham Wagstaff, who is a leading expert after studying the subject for almost 25 years. He believes that if cases were reported properly, without any sensation, then virtually all of the public concern would disappear.

There have been many 'problems' apparently caused by stage hypnosis. As fas as I am aware, all of them have now been discredited as having been caused by hypnosis. In fact the only provable case of injury I can find resulting from a show of stage hypnosis is a case in Glasgow where a participant fell off the stage and broke her leg because she was given the wrong instructions about how to leave for the toilet. This could have happened at any stage show, a pantomime or Royal Variety performance.

Are some practitioners doing tasteless shows?

Although what constitutes taste is subjective I believe some shows go beyond what is widely considered to be acceptable. Some night-clubs and pubs, mainly in the north of England, feature blue comedians and strippers and unfortunately also 'over the top' hypnotists. Often the participants have consumed large amounts of alcohol before the show. Their judgement is clouded and when the hypnotist asks them to remove items of clothing or participate in lurid sexual routines they oblige because of the alcohol and social pressure of the situation, not just because hypnosis is involved.

People do the same awful acts of exhibitionism in night-clubs simply encouraged by the disc-jockey, with no hypnotist in sight. Local licensing authorities should refuse licences for 'over the top' hypnotism shows though many of the shows in pubs and clubs are unlicensed in the first place.

Are the present regulations sufficient?

I believe they are. Since 1952 more than a million people have participated in stage hypnosis in the UK and there are no problems resulting from hypnosis itself. The existing act and Home Office guidelines are perfectly adequate. The only problem is that some licensing officers are not concerned enough to enforce the regulations. Whilst the vast majority of stage hypnotists are honourable professionals who apply for a licence, the disreputable performers often do not bother acquiring one. Just adding more regulations would I believe be futile. One only has to look at the fact that there are enormous regulations surrounding accountancy and politics, however, there are plenty of corrupt accountants and politicians and sadly always will be.

It is also obviously incredibly difficult to legislate against something that the psychological community cannot truly define and which some psychologists state doesn't even exist.

I believe that the only way to counter these ludicrous stories is by continuing to educate the public as to what hypnosis is. If people understand what it is then these sensational misperceptions can be ended once and for all.

MY FIVE WAYS TO STAY SAFE

Don't assume that every hypnotic show is the same as mine. There are an increasing number of rogues on the circuit who humiliate their subjects on stage for cheap laughs rather than tapping their imagination, giving a bad name to every good practitioner of hypnotism. If you are going to a public hypnotism show you are unsure about, it may be worth checking that it has been granted a licence under the 1952 Stage Hypnosis Act which means it will be closely monitored by officials from the local council. I never perform unless I can get a licence before each public show. If you are anxious about volunteering, here are five ways to make sure you stay safe:

1. Only volunteer to be hypnotised if you have seen the show before and trust the hypnotist. If you don't trust the hypnotist, for even the most minor reason, don't go on stage.
2. Never let yourself be hypnotised without friends present to see you are not taken advantage of.
3. Do not let yourself be hypnotised if you have been drinking. This can cloud your judgement.
4. Avoid hypnotists who tell their subjects to ignore pain with tricks such as 'rigid catalepsy'. This involves a volunteer lying between two chairs with no support for their back. They do not feel pain at the time, but it can cause immense problems to the spine and muscles.
5. Make sure the hypnotist or theatre has experienced medical back-up. Of course, there should be this with any form of public entertainment.

The Power of Hypnosis

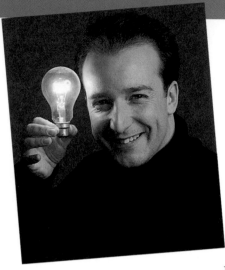

THERE is far more to the hypnotic world than making people pretend to be Mick Jagger or Michael Jackson. All the time I am hearing of amazing new examples of what hypnosis can do, ranging from a miracle cure for some problems to helping police solve serious crimes which had left them baffled.

I saw first hand and heard many fascinating accounts of the powers of hypnosis when I travelled around the world researching and filming a documentary on the subject for ITVs prestigious Network First slot in March 1995. I was lucky to team up with the highly acclaimed producers, Desmond Wilcox and Mike Latham, who was editor of Tomorrow's World and more particularly made the revolutionary James Burke shows in the 1970's.

Here are the most interesting cases I discovered on my travels along with other unusual, some now famous, uses of hypnosis. None, of course, should be tried at home!

PAIN CONTROL

Hypnosis is so powerful in pain control that many people have actually undergone major surgery using hypnotic suggestion as their only anaesthetic. Back in the nineteenth century Dr James Esdaile carried out hundreds of operations in India using hypnosis as the only anaesthetic. When he presented his case to the medical authorities of the day they arrogantly laughed at him.

I must admit I didn't really appreciate its effectiveness until taking part in an extraordinary experiment at the Virginia State University in Blacksburg in America. Psychology Professor Helen Crawford attached electrodes to my cheek and my scalp (through a bathing cap), so that she could measure the signals from my brain on a computer.

After putting me into trance she plunged my left hand into a bucket of ice-cold water. Before we started I could keep my hand in for only a few seconds before it became too painful. However, when in trance, Helen told me to forget about the ice and think of something else, the computer showed that my brain waves had changed and I was inhibiting the pain.

I concentrated on imagining a holiday I had taken at the Phuket Yacht Club in Thailand, laying in the sun looking out to the sea with Clare next to me. Amazingly, by reliving those vivid memories of a recent holiday, my brain started to bypass the pain, and that clearly showed up in my brain waves displayed on the computer.

Prof. Crawford told me to mark my pain level out of 10. Before the experiment it was definitely the full 10 when I had been forced to take my hand out, but now it was 3 going down to a 2. Even more surprising, when I came out of the trance, I thought my hand had been in the freezing water for a maximum of 15 seconds, Professor Crawford said it was in fact two minutes. Interestingly, one of the commonest trance phenomena is "time distortion".

'THE SNIP' – UNDER HYPNOSIS

Haircare consultant Andy Bryant hit the headlines when he had a vasectomy under hypnosis without anaesthetic and, immediately after the op, marched out, leapt in a cab and went to work.

Andy, a father of two, put himself in a trance just before the four minute operation to convince himself there would be no pain. He also told his body not to bleed which again, according to his surgeon Dr Tim Black, resulted in no blood being lost during the operation. He was conscious throughout and is the first Briton to have the surgery without pain killers.

Staff at the Marie Stopes clinic in London said patients usually hobble out afterwards, but apparently Andy simply went up a flight of stairs without even a grimace. Andy said: 'There was no pain and I continued with the day as if nothing had happened.

"I decided not to watch, but I could feel the knife going in. It was like being pinched but without the pain. I had switched off my body and told it there would be no pain." Dr Tim said he was astonished by his recovery. He said: 'He did flinch once and I told him not to worry. As soon as I told him to calm down he was fine. I was fascinated that he did not bleed. My biggest worry was that the hypnotist assisting him might faint, but he didn't."

HYPNOSIS IN MEDICINE

Surgeons used hypnosis in the 18th century, but the practice dwindled with the discovery of ether and chloroform. Unfortunately it dropped to the level of entertainment, but probably without stage hypnotists to keep the art alive it might have been forgotten altogether. However, now there are thought to be between 700 and 1,000 doctors and dentists using hypnosis in Britain, according to the British Society Of Medical and Dental Hypnotists and 2000 lay hypnotists.

In America nearly 20,000 physicians and psychologists use hypnosis according to the American Society of Clinical Hypnosis. It has been used in gall bladder operations, open heart surgery, impotency, burns, dentistry and painless childbirth. Skin disorders, stomach ulcers and stress-related migraines have all been found to respond well to hypnosis.

PAINLESS CHILDBIRTH

Hypnosis has been proven to help pregnant women have faster and easier births. Mums-to-be given a pre-natal course had a much happier delivery than women taking standard relaxation courses during the research.

Forty five volunteers were hypnotised during the 10 month project by GP Leslie Brann in Essex in 1987. To a background tape of crashing waves, the women were told they would feel less pain, have an easier delivery and recover more rapidly. They were even given the suggestion to fall asleep quickly at night after being woken by their babies.

After the course, first time mothers gave birth an average 90 minutes quicker than first timers among 51 women given normal relaxation classes. Women with previous children also had a shorter labour by an average of 40 minutes. Asked to give a one to ten enjoyment score, the hypnotised women rated the birth at an average of 7.4 compared to 5.6 for those in relaxation classes. Other recent research among women with fertility problems suggests that hypnotherapy can enhance chances of conception and reduce the risk of miscarriage.

BREAST ENLARGEMENT

Hypnotherapists in America are now inundated with female clients following controversy over the possible dangers of breast implants. Tests have shown that it is possible for women to increase their breast sizes purely by a course of hypnotherapy. It sounds incredible, but it is well documented that women who go through phantom pregnancies have enlarged breasts caused by the mind alone.

In fact, hypnotic techniques to improve breast size were first used in 1949 in an experiment with twenty women between the ages of 20 and 35. 17 out of the 20 women showed some increase in size from about one to one and a half inches and five showed growth of about two inches. In 1974 another study carried out on 13 women averaged an increase of around two inches.

CRACKING CRIME

I have used hypnosis to help police solve a crime involving manslaughter. In 1991, TV Production Manager Ian Brown witnessed a hit-and-run car crash. He saw a Fiat in Harrow, Middlesex, plough into and kill a cyclist, then speed off. After failing to completely recall the registration number, Ian came to me and, under hypnosis, wrote it down correctly. Acting on the information, police were able to track down and charge the hit-and-run driver who upon their arrival confessed and was eventually jailed.

Police in some parts of America have found hypnosis a highly successful method of tracking down dangerous criminals. Sometimes a victim of rape is too shocked to remember much of use to the police but under hypnosis the detectives sometimes find they can recall even minor distinguishing marks. The really amazing part is that a skilled forensic hypnotist will separate the memory of the event from the trauma associated with it so the witness doesn't mind recalling what happened.

ARTIST'S IMPRESSION

I visited San Francisco police HQ for my documentary and watched a demonstration of someone undergoing the forensic techniques. As she described her attacker to the police hypnotist, an artist painted his face. As you can see, the pictures which have been drawn while the victim was in trance bear a striking resemblance to the criminal as photograhped after the arrest. Of course, the drawback is that it is open to abuse because a person in a trance is vulnerable to any suggestion a police hypnotist makes. And despite its undeniable success, it is for this reason that police forces particularly in Britain are reluctant to turn to hypnosis in their battle against crime.

ARTIST'S IMPRESSION

HEALING WAYS

The power of the mind over the body is phenomenal. For 25 years, Elaine Simpson suffered from psoriasis. The uncomfortable and unsightly skin disease which causes itching and inflammation had been making her life a misery. But after she completed a 10 week course in hypnotherapy, she literally wiped away the ghastly sore which once covered almost 90 per cent of her body. You can see the amazing difference in the photographs taken before and after the treatment (left).

Elaine explained: "When I started having hypnotherapy, my body looked as though it was covered with third degree burns. I had resigned myself to having hospital treatment for the rest of my life. It was a nightmare." She added: "When I first decided to try hypnotism, I was nervous because I didn't want to lose control. But it was nothing like that. I just felt very calm and secure. "After about the sixth session the psoriasis started to disappear. It's amazing. Hypnotism has changed my life." Elaine was treated by one of Britain's most respected psychotherapists, Mandy Langford, at St Charles Hospital in West London in 1995. Mandy used hypnosis integrated with counselling to achieve the staggering results. She taught her how to make her mind control her body.

However, in 1952 a famous plastic surgeon Archibald McIndoe carried out extensive skin grafting on a boy who had a terrible skin disease in which the body is covered in warty scales. The grafts failed but then a senior registrar at the hospital tried hypnosis. It worked and the boy's skin cleared up and returned to normal. Only when others in the hospital started to express their amazement did the registrar discover that the disease was considered incurable. Subsequent attempts to hypnotise other sufferers failed to cure them, suggesting one of the most important components of hypnosis; that even though the subject need not believe the *hypnotist must.*

CAN HYPNOTISM CURE ILLNESS?

It is now being increasingly accepted in the West – they've accepted it in the East for years – that the mind can control the most complicated mechanisms of the body. I attended an experiment in an American infant school designed to see if we can control our immune system this way. If it is possible, there is hope that we perhaps could, in the future, effectively take on serious diseases.

A class of five-year-olds were shown a video featuring glove puppets representing the immune system and viruses. Then the kids were told to lie down, close their eyes and imagine policemen in their immune system, fighting germs inside their own bodies.

After 20 minutes saliva samples were taken and it was found that the children had elevated their levels of immunoglobulin A, an indication of heightened immune function.

It was clear they had boosted their immune systems just by using their imaginations in specific ways. The experiment has proved to be of lasting benefit and trials are now going on to see how it can help cancer sufferers.

READ 690,000 WORDS A MINUTE

Ever wanted to read a book in seconds? My colleague Paul Sheely has developed a way using a trance to make it possible for you to take in information at up to 690,000 words a *minute*. It is done by photographing the text of a page directly into the brain. Research has shown that anyone can learn to have an incredible memory and whilst photoreading is not a memory technique, it is a way of processing huge volumes of information very quickly. A good analogy would be a country view. Traditional reading is like looking at each tree, bush, cloud, etc individually one at a time. Photoreading is like looking at the scene all at once. Whilst you may miss the detail you appreciate the entire view.

Researcher Keith Fredericks, at the top computer centre Cray Research Institute in Minnesota, demonstrated a programme which has given people the ability to read at such an incredible speed. It is not like reading as we normally understand it.

He blends a 3D or 'Magic Eye' picture with a fast flowing text on a computer screen. While the conscious mind is captivated by the 3D picture, the unconscious mind takes in the scrolling text. I didn't know how true his claims were, but it is certainly a fact that the unconscious mind can process two million pieces of information every second.

I decided to put the program to the test myself. It was a very strange experience which made me feel a bit lightheaded. I sat in front of the screen for a minute watching words zip past my eyes.

I hadn't had time to take anything in at all, or so I thought, but when he started asking me questions about the book afterwards I couldn't believe how much I seemed to know.

I scored 73% which was statistically well in excess of anything I could have achieved just by guessing. It is pretty clear to me from this that we don't use anything like the full potential of our brains.

You don't need a computer to read the contents of a book at incredible speed. Paul Sheely teaches people to read a book while simply flicking through the pages, though he estimates that you only achieve a speed of 25,000 words like this. All this shows that the unconscious mind is stronger, and more mysterious, than most of us understand.

Stop Smoking NOW!

Ten million people in Britain – that is nearly 2,000 a day – have stopped smoking in the last 15 years. I believe it's easy to be one of them using hypnosis.

The reason people smoke is to change the way they feel. Essentially smokers are putting a smokescreen between themselves and their feelings. If you're a smoker, when you feel bored, frustrated or angry you tend to have a cigarette. You smoke on autopilot, mainly to control stress levels.

It is a really inefficient system.

Endorphins are the body's natural opiates that make you feel good and control pain. When you smoke, the chemicals from the cigarette interfere with that. So if you stop

MY SIX POINT PLAN TO STOPPING SMOKING FOR GOOD!

1 Decide the date you are going to quit and stick to it.
Tell at least three people you are going to stop on this date. Making such a public commitment has a powerful psychological effect on your mind.

2 Write down all the reasons why smoking is bad for you – make this personal to you.
For example: It's a dirty habit, it leaves yellow stains on my fingers and teeth, I smell disgusting, my breath stinks. Members of the opposite sex are put off. It's anti-social. It causes high blood pressure, heart disease, cancer. It costs a lot of money. Life insurance costs more. I hate giving over my will power to a drug. It makes me feel weak.

3 Write down the benefits you will get from stopping.
For example: People will like me better, I will save money, be more clearheaded. I will feel proud of myself and at ease with non smokers. I will look and smell clean and be free of fears for my health.

Hold the piece of paper and concentrate on imagining how good you'll look when you've stopped. Imagine saying: 'No thanks, I'm an ex-smoker." Even say it out loud.

Make the mental picture of your being a non-smoker big and bright and focus on it all the time. As you think of this image many times a day, you are continually reinforcing the change you have made.

you experience all your emotions more intensely. It's rather like walking through life with crutches and suddenly throwing them away – your legs feel a bit wobbly. That's why smokers who quit often go back to it.

BUT – over half of what smokers breathe in is fresh air and often one of the reasons smokers smoke is because they don't breathe properly. So the first thing to do when you quit, if you feel any pangs, is to take three deep breaths.

Next, sit down and make a list of reasons why it is a bad habit – it's dirty, expensive, socially unacceptable, unhealthy …

Associate pleasure to the idea of stopping – so tell yourself that when you have stopped you will feel more confident. You will feel a sense of victory about breaking the tyranny of nicotine. You will have more money which you can spend on something else and be more healthy.

Then imagine what it's like to be an ex-smoker. Go into trance and build up a clear mental picture of what it will be like not to smoke.

Some smokers might try to subvert your attempts because if you stop smoking it makes them feel powerless. They get a reflection of their own weakness so they might try to tempt you into just having one – if you do you're hooked all over again.

4 Break all your patterns of where and when you smoked. If you smoked in the car, take the ashtray out and clean the vehicle so it smells fresh.

5 Stop asking yourself why you can't stop smoking.
Build up your willpower by asking yourself these questions:
- How good will I feel when I've stopped smoking?
- What do I feel happiest about in my life?
- What am I most excited about or what would make me feel excited?
- What will I use my new wealth and fitness for?

Really think about and consider the answers until you feel better.

6 When the craving for nicotine strikes, breathe out deeply and deliberately, then relax and allow your body to take a big breath in. Do it three times. The extra oxygen in your blood makes you feel different fast – as fast as the effect of a cigarette used to be. Use this technique only when you really need it.

Remember only you can do it. Things will change as you put in the effort.
So make a commitment to yourself to do the techniques everyday.

Start now!

THE A-Z OF PHOBIAS

ACHLOPHOBIA – fear of crowds
ACROPHOBIA – fear of Heights
ARACHNOPHOBIA – fear of spiders
BRONTOPHOBIA – fear of storms
COPROPHOBIA – fear of faeces
CYNOPHOBIA – fear of dogs
EURYTHOPHOBIA – fear of blushing
GATOPHOBIA – fear of cats

HODOPHOBIA – fear of travel
NOSOPHOBIA – fear of illness
NYCTOPHOBIA – fear of darkness
PEDIOPHOBIA – fear of dolls
PHAGOPHOBIA – fear of swallowing
SCOPHOBIA – fear of being stared at
TRYPANOPHOBIA – fear of injections
ZOOPHOBIA – fear of animals

TOP FIVE PHOBIAS

FEMALE	MALE
Open spaces	Socialising
Small, closed spaces	Spiders
Spiders	Snakes
Snakes	Vertigo
Socialising	Small, closed spaces

Conquering phō′b|ĭas

phobia *n.* fear or aversion; unreasoning dislike

Spiders, heights, flying and even visits to the dentist – all are irrational fears that can make life hell for sufferers. While there is a variety of psychiatric treatments for phobias, some of them can take as much as six months to have any effect.

About five million Britons suffer from phobias and according to the Institute of Psychiatry they can strike three times as many women as men. Yet, remarkably, hypnosis can wipe out many debilitating fears in just minutes. One of the most common phobias is the fear of animals such as snakes and spiders. Some sufferers have told me that even watching them in a nature programme on TV can leave them practically paralysed with fear.

I have found one of the most effective techniques to overcome the fear is to tell the sufferer, under hypnosis, to picture in their mind the worst possible image of the creature they fear.

If it's a spider I then tell them to change the mental image of it. I encourage them to make fun of it. I get them to imagine anything

If this frightens you, turn the page and conquer your fear.

they like, the more ridiculous the better. If it is a tarantula, they could think of it wearing wellies, with a silly party hat on, blowing a bazooka, with bright orange hair and a clown's nose.

Fears can usually be dissolved through laughter as easily as that. I have known people who were once petrified of spiders happily hold them after simply changing the picture of them in their minds.

TV production assistant Martin Sole was hypnotised for a fear of spiders by my colleague Michael Breen on my ITV Network First documentary. After just a few sessions, his lifelong terror of creepy-crawlies had completely vanished. Where once he was paralysed with fear by just the sight of a tarantula on TV, now he could even feel relaxed enough about them to let one the size of a man's hand creep down his arm.

Martin, said: "I had been scared of spiders since I was a small boy. I had even turned down invitations to visit friends in Australia because they have bigger creepy crawlies over there. Then last year I found a spider on my lounge wall. Four hours and a few whiskies later I found the nerve to hit it with a plank of wood. That's when I realised my phobia was out of control.

''I decided to try hypnotherapy. At my first session, I was put in a trance and I was taught to regard spiders as something insignificant – not terrifying monsters. After the session I could hardly believe it when I picked up a tarantula. I just thought how small and harmless it seemed. Now I'm no longer scared of spiders. I just wish I had done this years ago."

Another all too common phobia is the fear of flying. One typical example was businesswoman Julia Obermajer-Navratil who, like many people, used to be so scared of flying she would down tranquillisers and a few drinks just to go on short trips. Longer haul flights were out of the question. But after just one session of hypnotherapy she suddenly found she enjoyed flying in a plane with the doors open.

The experiment to measure the effectiveness took place on a routine RAF training mission from RAF Lyneham in Wiltshire. It was immediately clear she had left her fear of flying on the ground because she didn't flinch when the loading doors were opened 25,000 feet up. In fact, she bravely walked down to the very edge of the gaping hole with the confidence of a born flier.

Julia said: "I used to loathe flying so much that I would get worried days before a flight which I had to do for business. When the plane started taxiing down the runway I was so scared I used to feel my heart was going to burst out of my chest.

"When my husband Joe went on business trips to Japan, I longed to join him. Then when my daughters wanted to fly to Florida like their friends, I had to explain it was my fault we couldn't go. In the end I decided to try hypnotism. During the treatment session I was hypnotised and told to replace my fear with something positive.

"A few days later, I met the film crew at RAF Lyneham and we took off in an RAF Hercules. Midway through the flight – at 20,000 ft – the rear door was opened. I shuffled over and instead of worrying about everything below, I thought about the glorious time I had once had ski-ing down a mountain. I felt so calm looking at the view. When we landed, I was so happy I kissed everyone in sight. It has made such a difference."

Another young woman, treated for a deep fear of heights, showed it had clearly worked by doing a bungee jump from a crane 180ft over the River Thames!

Gadgets: Eyeing up the Future

When I was younger my childhood ambition, as I have already mentioned, was to become a secret agent. I loved James Bond particularly because of all the amazing gadgets and devices he used. That probably goes some way to explaining my interest in the huge array of fascinating brain machines and self development devices now on sale.

I can understand that people might be put off this 'brain-boosting' technology, but I think it's a shame. It makes perfect sense to me that in these days where everybody is paying more attention to their physical fitness that we should also look to doing everything we can to improve our minds. The brain needs regular stimulation and challenge to function at its peak and it is easy to strengthen it through exercise - a kind of mind aerobics.

Mind machines provide this stimulation, they can also boost IQ, accelerate learning, improve memory, reduce stress by producing deep relaxation and enhance creativity. They can apparently even alleviate pain, overcome depression and increase sexual pleasure!

My only advice, if you have the chance to try any of them, is to closely follows the directions of how to use them; don't overdo it.

Brain Machines

Although there are many on the market, they mainly consist of goggles with a small series of stroboscopic lights that flash at a selected frequency that the brain switches to. They effectively change the brain's frequency in much the same way hypnosis does.

When you relax into trance there is an increase in theta waves which can be linked to super creativity and learning. Scientific research has shown that the theta state brings physical healing and re-generation along with a general increase in optimism.

One of the first machines of this type that I bought was the Photosonix Nova Pro which has various different settings for relaxation and meditation, sleep, learning and energizing. The machine consists of a control unit, red goggles and a set of stereo headphones. The lights in the goggles flash in synchronisation with a binaural pulse heard through stereo headphones that synchronise the left and right hemispheres of the brain.

These audio visual stimuli create an absorbing kaleidoscope of images and intriguing hallucinations appear as the brain tunes into the sound/light emissions from the little black box. I often use this machine for about 20 minutes, just before a show or during the interval, and when I take off the goggles and headphones I feel remarkably refreshed, relaxed and alert.

Brain machines electronically hypnotise you, tune up your brain and leave you feeling good and I believe that in the future there will be many more devices to change the way we feel and heal us.

The Alpha Stim

Stimulating the brain with electricity has been the subject of mountains of research over the last 40 years.

This machine consists of two small electrodes that attach to your ears and are connected to a small white box the size of a calculator. Inside it is a mini-computer that sends an electronic pulse to the brain that in turn creates an endorphin release.

Endorphins are the bodies natural opiates, they control pain and produce pleasure. You get them when you relax deeply, laugh a lot or after physical exercise - the joggers high. The type of endorphin release you get from the Alpha Stim creates a mild, though short-lasting, euphoria.

IBVA Scan

This is essentially a brain wave monitor. It consists of a headband with a tiny transmitter that sends to your computer an analysis of what brain waves you are emitting. When I was first wired up to this I found it absolutely amazing to be able to witness my thoughts displayed right in front of me in a pattern of brain waves.

Throughout time there has always been an interest in attaining peak states of mind particularly in the 1960's when many people tried to attain them chemically through drugs. However, there are drugless highs that come from meditation and recently scientists have carried out detailed studies of people meditating to see exactly what their brain is doing. The brain scan revealed that they were producing a lot of alpha and theta waves, which created these peak states.

Some researchers discovered that by watching the effect of their thinking on a monitor fed back to them, they were able to gain control over their brainwaves very quickly as well as many other autonomic processes, including blood pressure and heart rate. What took meditators years to learn was quickly available.

This technique is called 'bio-feedback'. By learning to use bio-feedback, you can become more relaxed, centred and healthy, as it gives you control over your thoughts and moods.

I think the time will come when people will sit in their offices, and instead of taking a mid morning coffee break they will alternatively reach for their brain machines. They sound, and look, like something from sci-fi movies, but these mind machines are just one of the incredible types of devices that are becoming part of a revolution in human development that has been growing for many years.

Mindrobics

I've designed a daily programme of exercises to help you achieve more of what you want in your life. Simply do whichever of them most appeals to you every day for about a month and remember to notice the changes in the way you feel. Everyone can use self hypnosis and visualisation techniques to change their whole outlook with a few simple steps.

HYPNOSIS FOR SELF CONFIDENCE

1 Sit down, close your eyes and remember a time when you felt really confident.

2 Picture in your mind what you saw, hear what you heard and feel what you felt. Now enhance those images. Make the pictures brighter and bolder, the colours richer, the sounds louder and the feelings stronger.

3 When you can feel a burst of that confidence quite strongly, carry out a specific action like squeezing your thumb and middle finger together. That will link in your mind the feeling of confidence with the finger squeeze.

4 Go through that routine ten times in a row to reinforce that link between your fingers and the feeling of confidence. Eventually it will mean that you will only have to squeeze your fingers together and you will begin to easily remember that confidence.

5 Now think about the event you want to be confident for. Imagine the event going as smoothly and as perfectly as you can while all the time squeezing your thumb and finger together re-triggering that confident feeling.

You will notice a difference in your confidence this time. Every time you do this you send a very strong message to your unconscious mind that you want to be more confident at that particular time in the future. I have known some people wipe out a life long fear of public speaking with this one simple exercise.

You cannot always change everything in your life immediately but you can certainly change the way that you perceive it. Success and happiness are not accidents that happen to some people and not to others. Success and happiness can be brought about by particular ways of behaving which are in turn determined by our ways of thinking. In other words it's not what happens to us that's important, but the way we choose to interpret it that shapes our lives.

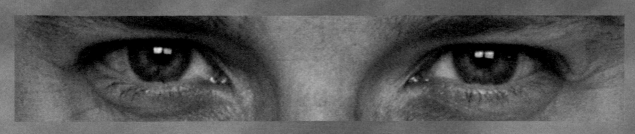

RUNNING YOUR OWN BRAIN

Here is one simple technique that I use regularly.

Close your eyes and think of something really good, either something that has happened or that you would like to happen. Now, make the colours brighter, the image bigger, bring it closer and turn the sound up louder. Notice what this does to your feelings. Doing this often will condition your unconscious mind to give you more of those good feelings, because you always get more of what you focus on in life.

For most people enhancing the size and colour of mental pictures does the same to the intensity of their feelings. Now try it the other way round with something mildly unpleasant. Close your eyes, think of something you don't like, drain the colour out, make it very small and move it off into the distance. It is interesting that by changing the images we see in our imagination we can literally change how we feel.

You can also play with auditory feedback. Notice the type of voice you use to criticise yourself with when you make a mistake, notice what it says, but particularly its' tone and location. Notice if it is at the front, back or to either side of your head.

Now move the location, imagine how that voice would sound talking to you from your shoulder, then from your elbow, then hear it talking from your wrist and eventually the tip of your thumb. You can also change the tone of it so it sounds like Mickey Mouse. Notice how that changes your feelings. Just because there's a voice inside your head doesn't mean you have to listen to it.

Negative self images can often become what psychologists call 'self-fulfilling prophecies'. People can end up sabotaging themselves because deep down they believe they are not worthy. I use a simple self hypnosis relaxation and imagination technique to heal the psychological scars of their poor self image.

By relaxing and imagining how you would ideally like to be, over and over again every morning, you can begin to change, to reprogramme yourself and become more positive, optimistic, healthy, energised, motivated, confident and enthusiastic.

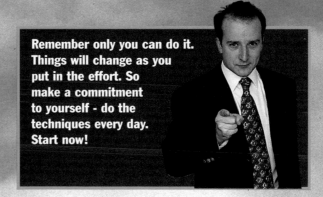

Remember only you can do it. Things will change as you put in the effort. So make a commitment to yourself - do the techniques every day. Start now!

91

More things you never  *knew*

There used to be an ITV rule banning hypnosis programmes altogether.

Hypnotists were brought in by supermarket chain ASDA in 1993 to help staff quit smoking at its Leeds headquarters.

A family in Aintree, Liverpool had their pet doberman dog hypnotised to stop him howling and whining in the night – it apparently worked.

Mark Knopfler of Dire Straits fame reportedly beat his 40 a day, 30 year smoking habit through hypnosis.

about

Hypnotherapy was commended in the House of Lords on November 20, 1979 as a useful technique which would not benefit from restrictions.

At a Home Office Conference in 1982 a Doctor from Surrey University said he had hypnotised more than 100 people mainly on behalf of the police.

hypnosis

The ancient druids called hypnosis "magic sleep" and used it to cure warts and cast spells.

Bill Steeds of Sacramento, USA makes £50,000 a year training frogs for jumping contests by apparently hypnotising them.

Lily Tomlin is said to have written the screenplay for "The incredible Shrinking Woman" while in an hypnotic trance.

"Sexnotherapist" Dr Rachel Copelan uses hypnosis in her practice in Beverly Hills to help couples with sexual and relationship problems.

Hypnosis of witnesses and suspects was first used seriously by the Israelis to get evidence in terrorist cases.

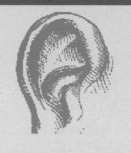

Sleep like a log

COUNTING sheep isn't the easiest way to get to sleep as anyone who has lain in bed for hours trying to get to sleep will tell you.

There is a way to learn to use your brain more effectively that will ensure a good night's sleep. I have developed six golden rules that have helped thousands of insomniacs get a decent night's sleep which are included on my Hypnotherapy tape Sleep Like A Log.

I guarantee it is much better for you than taking sleeping pills and it will also last considerably longer without any of the negative side effects. Once your sleep pattern has been established you will wake up refreshed and ready for anything.

MY SIX POINT PLAN FOR A GOOD NIGHT'S SLEEP

1 Get up half an hour earlier than usual and make sure you stick to it every day – even Sundays.

2 Go to bed only when you feel sleepy. This will soon tend to happen at a regular time.

3 Bed is for sleeping – or making love. Don't get in the habit of using it to lounge on while reading, eating or watching TV.

4 If you are still awake 40 minutes after going to bed, get up and do something boring like the ironing. When your unconscious mind associates being awake at night with tedious tasks, it will become motivated to induce sleep.

5 Do not take naps or rest with your eyes closed during the day. That will only disrupt your natural sleep cycle.

6 Sort out your worries during the day. Putting it off triggers your unconscious mind at bedtime. One of the common reasons for insomnia is worrying. Using the plans on Controlling Stress and Achieving Success (pages 26 and 62) can also help you to stop worrying.

Behind every concern about what you don't want is something you do want. For example, not wanting an overdraft means you do want money in the bank. Focus on what you desire. Work out how to get it, step by step. Taking one step each day means it will be easier to sleep, knowing you are on your way to your goal. If you wake up in the middle of the night worrying, believe it or not your mind is trying to help you, it's alerting your attention to something, only not at a particularly good time.

Remember only you can do it. Things will change as you put in the effort.
So make a commitment to yourself to do the techniques everyday.

Start now!

IT'S EASY WITH HYPNOTHERAPY

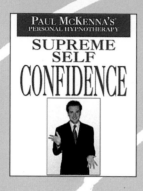

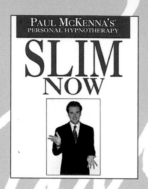

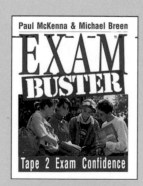

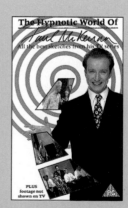

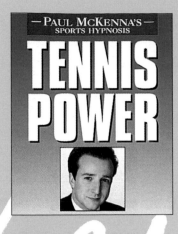

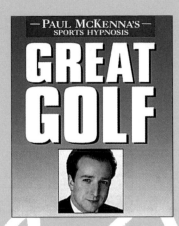

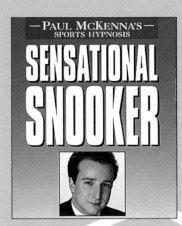

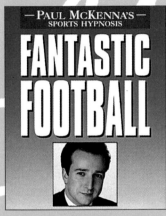

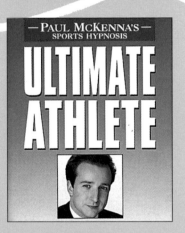

To obtain a copy of any one of my successful Hypnotherapy tapes, my first book, The Hypnotic World of Paul McKenna, or my video (which contains all the best routines from The Hypnotic World of Paul McKenna TV series, plus footage not shown on TV) Please send a stamped, self-addressed envelope for an order form to the following address;

PAUL McKENNA PRODUCTIONS
PO BOX 5514 · LONDON · W8 4LY

Paul McKenna

Acknowledgements

I would like to thank, for their help in making this book possible,

Dave Hogan, Trevor Leighton, Hugh Willbourn, Dennis Edensor, Marion Morgan,
Caroline Hogan, Kate Davey, Matthew Ashenden, Tom Johnston, Biff, Dennis Selinger,
Pete Wilson at Harvey Goldsmith, Michael Breen, Stuart Higgins at the *Sun*, Kate Staples,
Nigel Benn, Bobby Davro, Esther Rantzen, Robin Smith, Iain Dowie, Frank Bruno, Paula Yates,
Murray Buesst at Carlton TV, Kris Thykier, Jonathan Brown, Elizabeth 'ER' Richards,
Joan McKenna, Melanie Ellis, Humphrey Price and of course 2 Birds Atit.

You are welcome to write to me. For a reply, please ensure you enclose
a stamped self-addressed envelope. My office address is:

PAUL McKENNA PRODUCTIONS
PO BOX 5514 · LONDON · W8 4LY

Alternatively, if you want the name of a qualified and reputable
hypnotherapist in your area please contact:

MANDY LANGFORD
ST CHARLES HOSPITAL · EXMOOR STREET · LONDON · W10 6DZ
or TELEPHONE 0181 964 1206

If you would like to find out more about hypnosis my first book *The Hypnotic
World of Paul McKenna* has an extensive recommended reading list.

Paul McKenna